Math in FOCUS®

Singapore Math®
by Marshall Cavendish

Student Edition

Program Consultant and Author
Dr. Fong Ho Kheong

Authors
Chelvi Ramakrishnan
Michelle Choo

U.S. Distributor

Houghton Mifflin Harcourt.
The Learning Company™

Marshall Cavendish
Education

Grade
2B

Contents

Chapter

8 Multiplication and Division

Chapter Opener

What are the different ways to multiply
and divide?

RECALL PRIOR KNOWLEDGE
Adding different groups

▶ Hands-on Activity

Multiplication Tables

▶ Hands-on Activity

Chapter

Time and Money

Chapter Opener

197

How can you tell time in different ways? When do you use addition and subtraction in money?

RECALL PRIOR KNOWLEDGE
198

Skip counting by 5s and 10s • Finding numbers in a pattern by adding or subtracting • Telling time • Types of coins • Exchanging coins • Combining coins to show a given amount

▶ Hands-on Activity

Manipulative List

10-sided die

Attribute block tray

Clock

Coin set

Connecting cubes

Geometric solids

Paper money

Transparent counters

Preface

Welcome!

Math in Focus® is a program that puts **you** at the center of an exciting learning experience! This experience is all about helping you to really understand math and become a strong and confident problem solver!

What is in your book?

Each chapter in this book begins with a real-world example of the math topic you are about to learn.

In each chapter, you will see these features:

THINK provides a problem for the whole section, to get you thinking. If you cannot answer the problem right away, you can come back to it a few times as you work through the section.

ENGAGE contains tasks that link what you already know with what you will be learning next. You can explore and discuss the tasks with your classmates.

LEARN introduces you to new math concepts using examples and activities, where you can use objects to help you learn.

Hands-on Activity gives you the chance to work closely with your classmates, using objects or drawing pictures, to help you learn math.

TRY gives you the chance to practice what you are learning, with support.

INDEPENDENT PRACTICE allows you to work on different kinds of problems, and to use what you have learned to solve these problems on your own.

Additional features include:

RECALL PRIOR KNOWLEDGE	 Math Talk	MATH SHARING	GAME
Helps you recall related concepts you learned before, accompanied by practice questions	Invites you to talk about your thinking and communicate your ideas to your classmates and teachers	Encourages you to create strategies, discover methods, and share them with your classmates and teachers using mathematical language	Helps you to really master the concepts you learned, through fun partner games
LET'S EXPLORE	**MATH JOURNAL**	**PUT ON YOUR THINKING CAP!**	**CHAPTER WRAP-UP**
Extends your learning through investigation	Allows you to reflect on your learning when you write down your thoughts about the concepts learned	Challenges you to apply the concepts to solve problems in different ways	Summarizes your learning in a flow chart and helps you to make connections within the chapter
CHAPTER REVIEW	**Assessment Prep**	**PERFORMANCE TASK**	**STEAM**
Provides you with a lot of practice in the concepts learned	Prepares you for state tests with assessment-type problems	Assesses your learning through problems that allow you to demonstrate your understanding and knowledge	Promotes collaboration with your classmates through interesting projects that allow you to use math in creative ways

Let's begin your exciting learning journey with us! Are you ready?

Chapter 7

Graphs and Line Plots

Let's record our measurements in a tally chart. How can we represent the data in a graph?

Height (inches)	Tally	Number of Seedlings
1	IIII	
2	₩₩	
3		
4		

How can you collect data?
How can you represent the data collected in different ways?

Name: _____   Date: _____

Collecting and organizing data

Melanie has some toy animals.

The picture graph shows the number of toy animals Melanie has.

Toy Animals Melanie Has

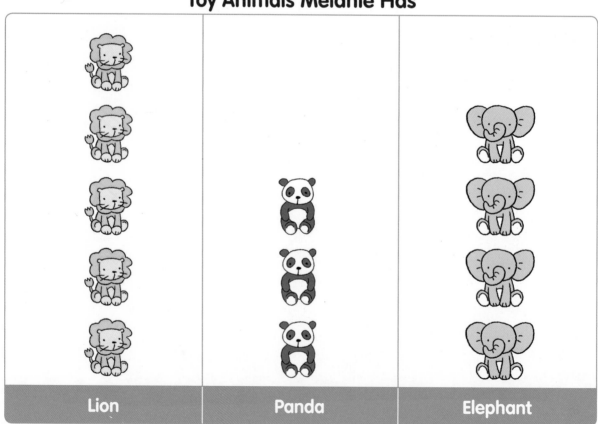

| Lion | Panda | Elephant |

a   She has 4 elephants.

b   She has 1 more lion than elephants.

c   She has 2 fewer pandas than lions.

d   She has the most number of lions.

e   She has the fewest number of pandas.

f   She has a total of 12 toy animals.

Melanie draws a tally chart using this data.

Toy Animal	Tally	Number of Toy Animals
Lion	⁙|	5
Panda	|||	3
Elephant	||||	4

Melanie draws a picture graph using this data.

She uses ☐ to stand for 1 toy animal.

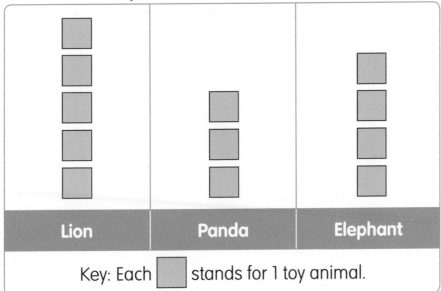

Toy Animals Melanie Has

Key: Each ☐ stands for 1 toy animal.

▶ **Quick Check**

A group of children goes to Winter Funland.

The picture graph shows the number of children playing each activity.

Activities Children Play

	Snowboarding	 👤 👤 👤 👤 👤
	Skiing	 👤 👤 👤
	Snow Tubing	 👤 👤 👤 👤 👤 👤

Fill in each blank.

1 There are _____ children snowboarding.

2 There are _____ children skiing.

3 The most popular activity is _____.

4 _____ fewer children are skiing than snowboarding.

5 _____ more children are snow tubing than skiing.

6 There are _____ children at Winter Funland in all.

Complete the tally chart.

7

Type of Activities	Tally	Number of Children
Snowboarding		
Skiing		
Snow Tubing		

Use the tally chart in **7** to make a picture graph.

Use ◯ to stand for 1 child.

8

Activities Children Play

| Snowboarding | Skiing | Snow Tubing |

Key: Each ◯ stands for 1 child.

 # Picture Graphs

Learning Objectives:
• Collect data and draw picture graphs.
• Read, analyze, and interpret data in picture graphs.

New Vocabulary
survey

 **THINK**

a Peyton has 2 toy cars, 1 robot, 3 dolls, and 1 dollhouse.
Show the data in a graph.

b She wants at least 1 more toy car than the other toys in all.
How many more toy cars should she buy?
Show the data in a graph.

What information do I know?
What do I need to find out?

ENGAGE

Look around your classroom.
How many students have:

a brown eyes?

b blue eyes?

c green eyes?

Show how you can make a tally chart to show your data.
What other ways can you show your data?

LEARN Make and read picture graphs

1 Camila carried out a survey to collect some data.
She asked 10 classmates to choose their favorite color.
She recorded her data in a tally chart.

Color	Tally
Red	|||
Blue	||||
Green		
Yellow	||

Then, Camila used the data to draw a picture graph.

Favorite Colors

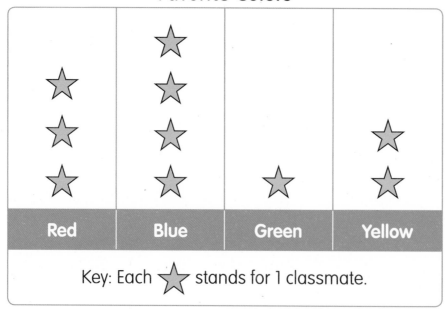

Key: Each ⭐ stands for 1 classmate.

A total of 7 classmates chose red or blue.

The total number of classmates who chose red or green is the same as the number of classmates who chose blue.

The number of classmates who chose blue is 1 more than the total number of classmates who chose green or yellow.

2 Amy asked her classmates to choose their favorite class. She recorded her data in the picture graph.

Favorite Classes

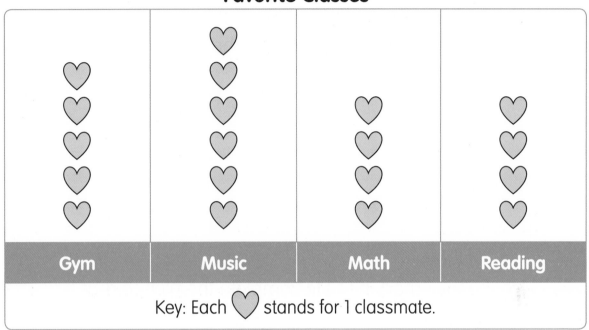

Key: Each ♡ stands for 1 classmate.

a How many classmates chose Math or Reading?

4 classmates chose Math.
4 classmates chose Reading.

4 + 4 = 8

8 classmates chose Math or Reading.

b How many more classmates chose Math or Reading than Music?

8 classmates chose Math or Reading.
6 classmates chose Music.

8 − 6 = 2

2 more classmates chose Math or Reading than Music.

A total of 14 classmates chose three of the classes. Which are the three possible classes?

Hands-on Activity Collecting data to make a picture graph

(1) Make a list of four possible snacks.

(2) Conduct a survey to find out what your classmates' favorite snacks are.
Then, record your data in the tally chart.

Snack	Tally

(3) Use the tally chart in (2) to complete the picture graph.

Favorite Snacks

Key: Each _____ stands for 1 classmate.

(4) Write a question from the picture graph.
Get your partner to answer the question.

Your question:

_____

Your partner's answer:

_____

© 2020 Marshall Cavendish Education Pte Ltd

TRY Practice making and reading picture graphs

Complete the tally chart.

Scarlett, Jose, Aaron, and Victoria baked some cookies.
The tally chart shows the number of cookies each person baked.

1

Name	Tally	Number of Cookies
Scarlett	卌 卌 ‖	
Jose	卌 ‖‖	
Aaron	卌 卌 卌 ‖	
Victoria	卌 卌	

Use the tally chart in ① to make a picture graph.
Use ♥ to stand for 1 cookie.

2

Number of Cookies Baked

Scarlett	**Jose**	**Aaron**	**Victoria**

Key: Each _____ stands for 1 cookie.

Look at the picture graph.
Then, fill in each blank.

The picture graph shows the storybooks that a group of children like.

Storybooks a Group of Children Like

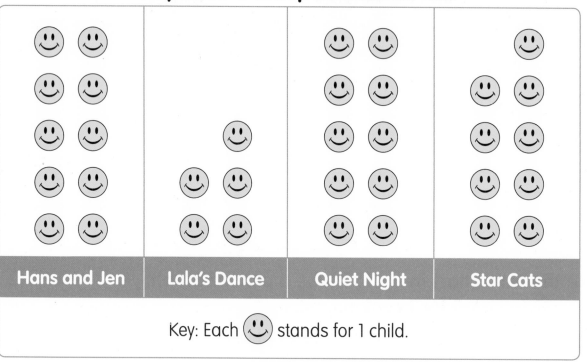

Key: Each 😊 stands for 1 child.

3 The same number of children like _____ and
   _____.

4 _____ children like Lala's Dance or Star Cats.

5 There are _____ children in all.

6 _____ more children like Hans and Jen or Quiet Night
   than Lala's Dance or Star Cats.

7 Another 4 children like Hans and Jen.
   _____ children like Hans and Jen now.

INDEPENDENT PRACTICE

Look at the picture graph.
Then, answer each question.

The picture graph shows the flowers in Van's garden.

Flowers in Van's Garden

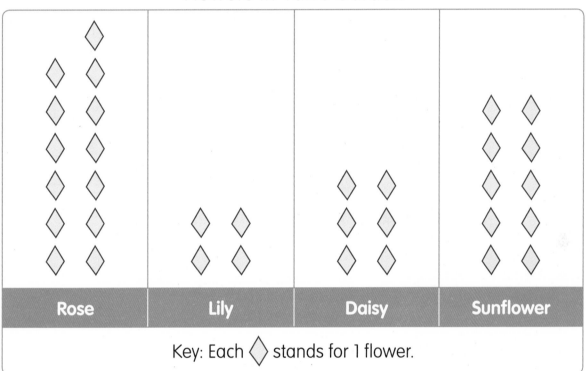

Key: Each ◇ stands for 1 flower.

1. How many flowers are there in all? _____

2. How many flowers are **not** roses? _____

3. How many fewer lilies than sunflowers are there? _____

4. How many more roses than lilies and daisies are there?

   _____

5. The total number of two types of flowers is the same as the number of sunflowers.
   Which are the two types of flowers?
   _____ and _____

Read the conversation to make a picture graph.
Use △ to stand for 1 apple.

I have 6 green apples.

I have 2 green apples and 4 red apples.

Raccoon and I have 9 apples in all.

I have 1 apple more than the total number of apples Raccoon and Hedgehog have.

6

Number of Apples Each Animal Has

Raccoon	
Bear	
Hedgehog	
Fox	

Key: Each ____ stands for 1 apple.

Use the picture graph in ⑥ to answer each question.

7 _____ and _____ have the same number of apples.

8 Raccoon and Bear have _____ apples in all.

9 Bear has _____ more apples than Hedgehog.

10 Fox and Hedgehog have _____ more apple than Raccoon and Bear.

11 The animals have _____ apples in all.

2 Bar Graphs

Learning Objectives:
• Collect data and draw bar graphs.
• Read, analyze, and interpret data in bar graphs.

New Vocabulary
vertical bar graph
scale
axis
horizontal bar graph

THINK

A group of students chose their favorite fruit.
The result was recorded in a tally chart.

Fruit	Tally
Apple	卌 ||||
Orange	卌 卌 ||
Peach	卌 |||
Watermelon	卌 卌 |

a   How can you show the data in a graph in two ways?

b   Some of the students changed their choices.

   i   5 students chose watermelon instead of peach.

   ii   3 students chose peach instead of apple.

What will the final graph look like?

ENGAGE

Ask your classmates what their favorite sport is.
Use a tally chart to show your findings.
Your teacher will give you strips of paper.
Use the strips of paper to make a bar graph to show the data.

LEARN Make and read bar graphs

1 Valeria counted the number of flowers on 4 plants A, B, C, and D. She recorded the information in a tally chart.

Plant	Tally
A	|
B	卌 ||
C	卌
D	|||

She drew a picture graph to show the information.

Flowers on Four Plants

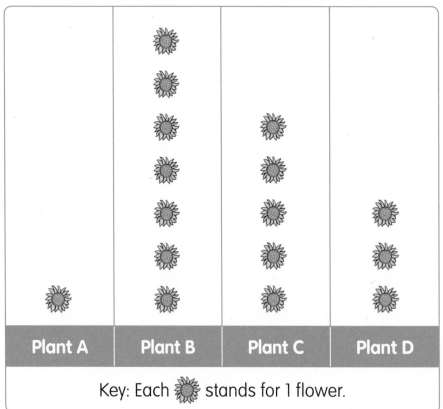

Key: Each 🌻 stands for 1 flower.

She also drew a vertical bar graph to show the same information.
A scale shows the value of the bars.
In this graph, the vertical axis or grid line is marked 1, 2, 3, 4, 5, 6, 7, and 8.
These markings represent the scale.

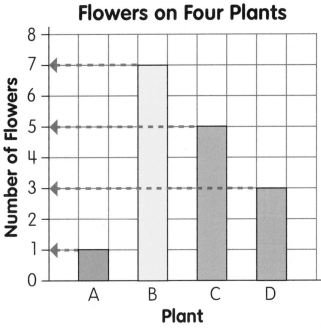

Flowers on Four Plants

The number of flowers can be read from the scale of the graph.

Like a picture graph, a bar graph is also useful for comparing data.

Math Talk

Breakfasts Taken

Adrian says that most students take pancakes for breakfast as the length of the bar for pancake is the longest.
Do you agree?
Why?

2 Ayden drew a horizontal bar graph.
This bar graph shows the number of animals on a farm.

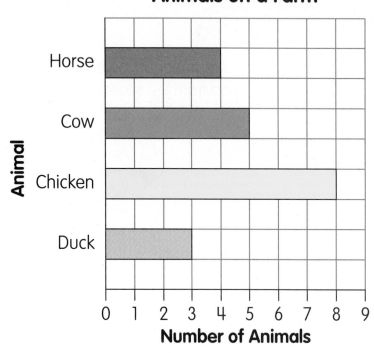

Animals on a Farm

a How many animals are there on the farm in all?
4 + 5 + 8 + 3 = 20
There are 20 animals on the farm in all.

b How many animals are **not** horses?
5 + 8 + 3 = 16
There are 16 animals that are not horses.

c How many fewer ducks than chickens are there?
8 – 3 = 5
There are 5 fewer ducks than chickens.

What is another way to find the answer?

d How many more cows than ducks are there?

$5 - 3 = 2$

There are 2 more cows than ducks.

e Compare the number of chickens to the total number of horses and cows.
How many more?

$4 + 5 = 9$

The total number of horses and cows is 9.

$9 - 8 = 1$

The total number of horses and cows is 1 more than the number of chickens.

Hands-on Activity Collecting data to make a bar graph

(1) Make a list of four possible favorite places to go.

(2) Have your classmates choose a favorite place.
Then, record your data in the tally chart.

Place	Tally

③ Use the tally chart in ② to draw a bar graph.

Favorite Places

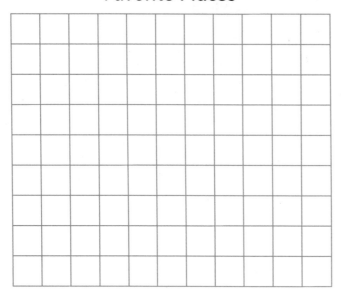

④ Write a question from the bar graph.
Get your partner to answer the question.

Your question:

_____

Your partner's answer:

_____

TRY Practice making and reading bar graphs

The tally chart shows the pets Brooke's classmates keep.

Pet	Tally
Rabbit	卌 ||||
Bird	||||
Fish	卌
Cat	卌 ||

**Use the tally chart to complete the bar graph.
Then, answer each question.**

1   **Pets Brooke's Classmates Keep**

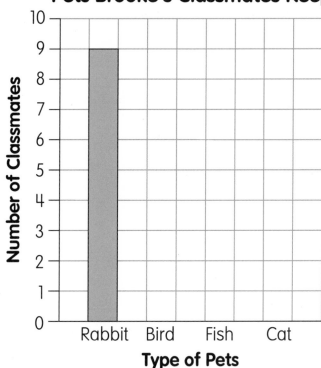

2 How many classmates keep pets? _____

3 How many classmates do **not** keep fish as pets? _____

4 How many more classmates keep cats than birds
as pets? _____

5 How many fewer classmates keep fish than rabbits
as pets? _____

6 The number of classmates who keep rabbits as pets is the
same as the number of classmates who keep two other
types of pets.
Which are the two other types of pets?

_____ and _____

Look at the bar graph.
Then, fill in each blank.

The bar graph shows the number of books read by four children.

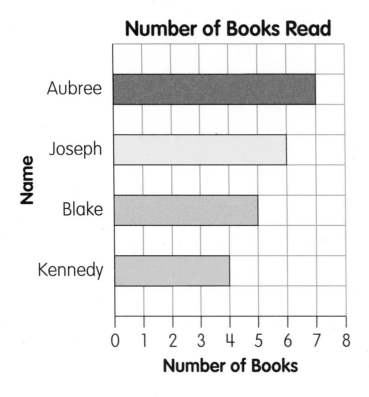

Number of Books Read

Name

Number of Books

7 The children read _____ books in all.

8 Aubree read _____ more books than Kennedy.

9 Joseph and Kennedy read _____ more books than Blake.

10 Blake and Kennedy read _____ fewer books than Aubree
and Joseph.

11 Aubree and _____ read the same number of books as

Joseph and _____ .

Name: _____   Date: _____

INDEPENDENT PRACTICE

Look at the bar graph.
Then, answer each question.

The bar graph shows the favorite fruit juices of a group of children.

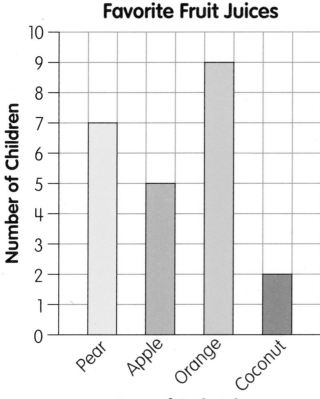

Favorite Fruit Juices

Number of Children

Type of Fruit Juices

1. How many children were there in all? _____

2. How many children did **not** choose pear juice? _____

3. How many more children chose orange juice than apple juice
   or coconut juice? _____

4. The number of children who chose pear juice is the same as the
   number of children who chose two other fruit juices.
   Which two fruit juices were chosen?

   _____ and _____

Look at the bar graph.
Then, fill in each blank.

The bar graph shows the number of hours Ms. Flores babysat.

Number of Hours Ms. Flores Babysat

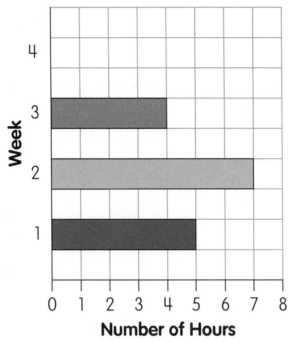

5 Ms. Flores babysat 4 hours more in Week 4 than in Week 3. Complete the bar graph for Week 4.

6 Ms. Flores babysat for _____ hours in four weeks.

7 Ms. Flores babysat _____ hours more in Week 2 than in Week 1.

8 Ms. Flores babysat 1 hour less in Week 2 than in Week _____.

9 The total number of hours Ms. Flores babysat in Weeks
_____ and _____ is the same as the total number
of hours in Weeks _____ and _____.

10 Ms. Flores babysat a total of 31 hours in five weeks.
She babysat _____ hours in Week 5.

3 Line Plots

Learning Objectives:
• Collect data and draw line plots.
• Read, analyze, and interpret data in line plots.

New Vocabulary
line plot

 THINK

The graph shows the height of 6 plants in centimeters.

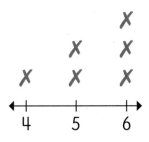

What do the numbers and ✗ mean?

ENGAGE

Measure each line.
Then, record the data.

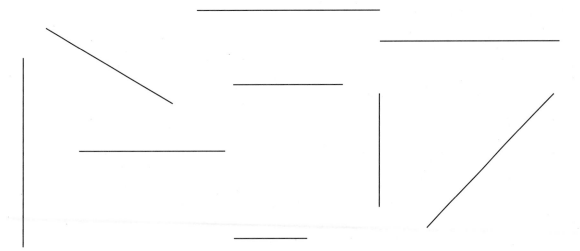

Besides using a bar graph, what is another way to show the data?

LEARN Make and read line plots

1. Elijah measures the length of some leaves.

Leaf	A	B	C	D	E	F	G	H	I
Length (inches)	2	3	4	2	3	2	2	1	2

Then, he records his data in a tally chart.

Length (inches)	Tally	Number of Leaves
1	|	1
2	‖‖	5
3	‖	2
4	|	1

Elijah shows the data using a bar graph.

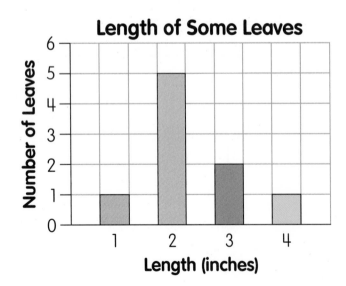

Elijah also uses the data to draw a line plot.

A line plot shows data on a number line.
The **x** shows how often something happens.

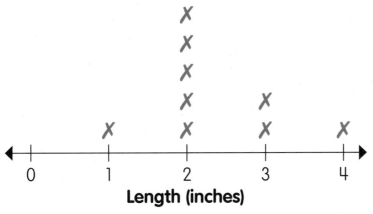

Length (inches)

Key: Each **x** stands for 1 leaf.

One **x** means 1 leaf has a length of 1 inch.

Five **x** means 5 leaves have a length of 2 inches each.

a   How many leaves have a length of 3 inches?
2 leaves have a length of 3 inches.

b   How many leaves have a length of 4 inches?
1 leaf has a length of 4 inches.

c   How many leaves have a length of at least 3 inches?
3 leaves have a length of at least 3 inches.

d   How many leaves have a length of at most 3 inches?
8 leaves have a length of at most 3 inches.

e   How many leaves have a length of 2 inches or less?
6 leaves have a length of 2 inches or less.

f   How many leaves are there in all?
There are 9 leaves in all.

Hands-on Activity Measuring objects to make a line plot

Work in groups.

1. Find four objects less than 4 inches on your desk or in your classroom.

2. Measure the length of each object to the nearest inch. Then, record your data in the table.

Object	Length (inches)

3. Collect the measurements from two other classmates. Then, record all your data in the tally chart.

Length (inches)	Tally	Number of Objects
1		
2		
3		
4		

④ Use the tally chart in ③ to draw a line plot.

Length (inches)

Key: Each ✗ stands for 1 object.

⑤ Answer each question.

a How many objects are about 2 inches long? _____

b How many objects are about 4 inches long? _____

c What is the length with the greatest number of objects?
   about _____ inches

d How many objects were measured in all? _____
   How do you know? _____

TRY Practice making and reading line plots

Complete the tally chart.

Xavier measured the length of some sticks.

Length (inches)	Tally	Number of Sticks
1	||	
2	卌	
3	卌 卌||	
4	|||	

Use the tally chart in ① to complete the bar graph.

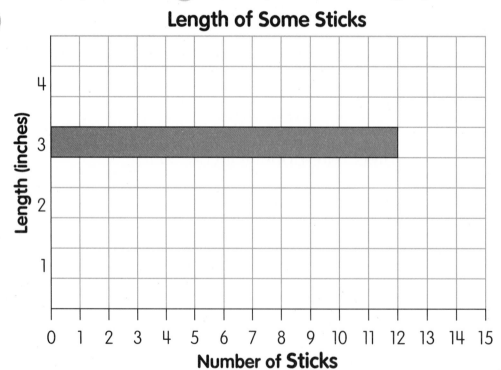

Length of Some Sticks

Xavier also used the data to draw a line plot.

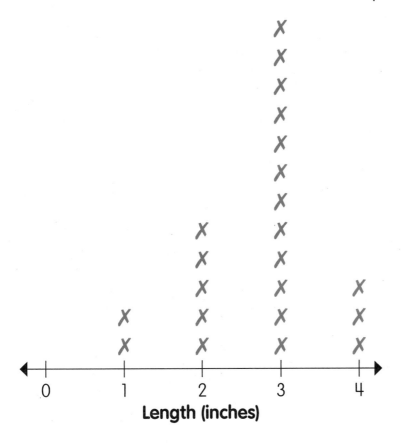

Length (inches)

Fill in each blank.

3. Each ✗ stands for 1 _____.

4. Five ✗ means _____ sticks have a length of 2 inches each.

5. The greatest number of sticks have a length of _____ inches each.

6. _____ sticks have a length of at most 3 inches each.

7. There are _____ sticks in all.

Look at the line plot.
Then, answer each question.

Dominic measured the length of some pieces of string.

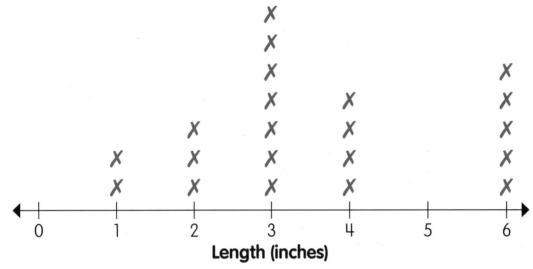

Key: Each ✗ stands for 1 piece of string.

8 How many pieces of string have a length of 6 inches each?

_____

9 How many pieces of string have a length of at least 4 inches each?

_____

10 How many pieces of string have a length of 3 inches or more?

_____

11 How many pieces of string have a length of less than 3 inches each?

_____

12 How many pieces of string are there in all? _____

INDEPENDENT PRACTICE

Complete the tally chart.

1 Ms. Taylor measured the height of her flowers in her garden. Then, she recorded her data in a tally chart.

Height (inches)	Tally	Number of Flowers
10	卌	
11	卌 IIII	
12	卌 卌 I	
13	III	

Use the tally chart in ① to complete the bar graph.

2

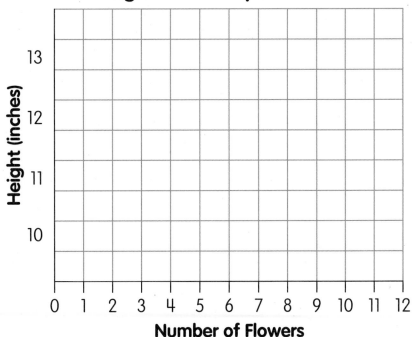

Height of Ms. Taylor's Flowers

**Complete the line plot to show the data on the previous page.
Then, answer each question.**

Height (inches)

④ What do the ✗s on the line plot stand for?

_____

⑤ How many ✗s are marked on the line plot? _____

⑥ How many flowers have a height of 12 inches or more?

_____

⑦ How many flowers have a height of at least 11 inches?

_____

⑧ What is the height of the fewest number of flowers?

_____ inches

Name: _____ Date: _____

Mathematical Habit 4 Model with mathematics

Find what your classmates' favorite seasons are.
Record your data in the tally chart.

Season	Tally
Spring	
Summer	
Fall	
Winter	

Then, draw a bar graph to show the data.

Favorite Seasons

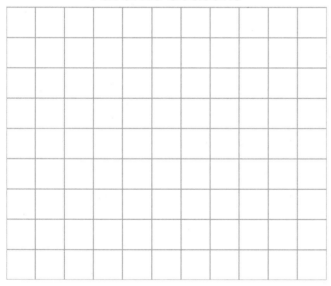

Write statements about your data using
'greatest/fewest number of classmates'
and 'more/fewer than'.

_____

_____

Problem Solving with Heuristics

1 **Mathematical Habit 2** Use mathematical reasoning

There are 17 students in Mr. Hill's class.

2 of the students have 2 siblings.

5 of the students are the only child.

10 of the students have 2 or fewer siblings.

9 of the students have 2 or more siblings.

The greatest number of siblings that a student has is 3.

The total number of children in all the families is 45.

Look at the picture graphs.
Then, answer each question.

Picture Graph A:

Number of Siblings Each Student Has

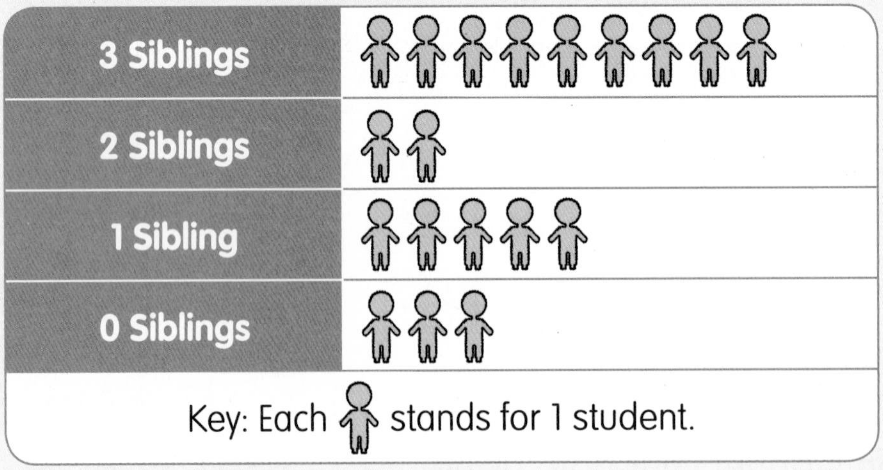

3 Siblings	👤👤👤👤👤👤👤👤👤
2 Siblings	👤👤
1 Sibling	👤👤👤👤👤
0 Siblings	👤👤👤

Key: Each 👤 stands for 1 student.

© 2020 Marshall Cavendish Education Pte Ltd

Picture Graph B:

**Number of Siblings
Each Student Has**

3 Siblings	👤👤👤👤👤👤👤
2 Siblings	👤👤
1 Sibling	👤👤👤
0 Siblings	👤👤👤👤👤

Key: Each 👤 stands for 1 student.

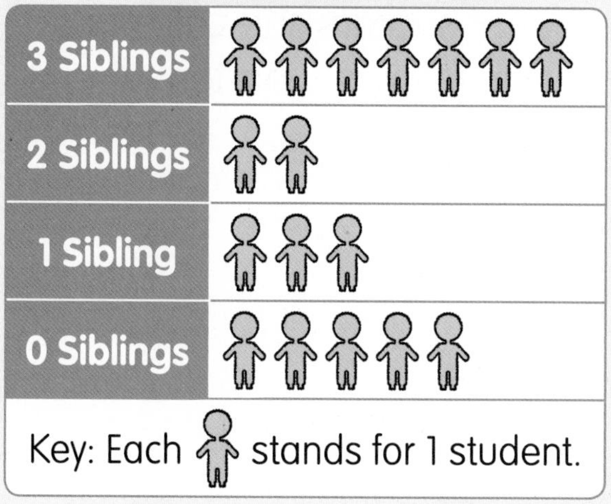

Picture Graph C:

**Number of Siblings
Each Student Has**

3 Siblings	👤👤👤👤👤👤👤
2 Siblings	👤👤
1 Sibling	👤👤👤👤👤👤👤👤
0 Siblings	👤👤👤👤👤

Key: Each 👤 stands for 1 student.

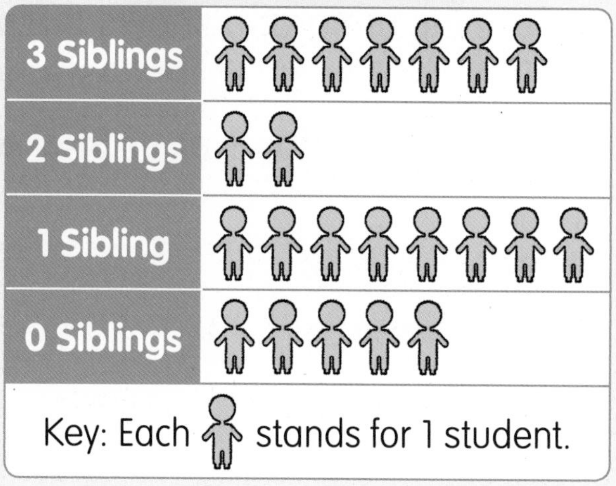

a   Which of the following picture graphs correctly represents the given data?

b   Why are there 45 children in all the families?

2 **Mathematical Habits 8** **Look for patterns**

Ashanti records the number of stickers she collects every day for 4 days. The picture graph shows the number of stickers she collects. The number of stickers Ashanti collects follows a pattern.

Number of Stickers Ashanti Collects

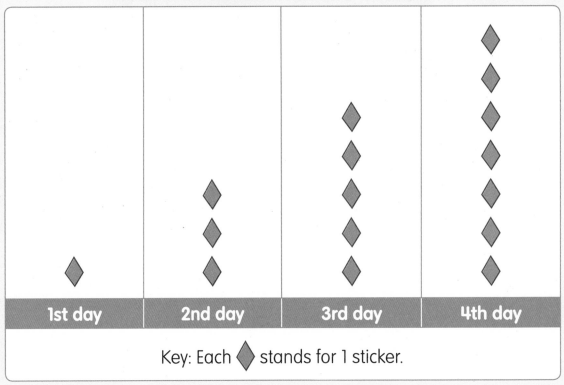

Key: Each ◆ stands for 1 sticker.

If this pattern carries on,

a   How many stickers will Ashanti collect on the 5th day?

Ashanti will collect _____ stickers on the 5th day.

b   How many stickers will Ashanti collect on the 6th day?

Ashanti will collect _____ stickers on the 6th day.

c   How many stickers will Ashanti collect on the 7th day?

Ashanti will collect _____ stickers on the 7th day.

CHAPTER WRAP-UP

Graphs and Line Plots

Picture Graphs

A picture graph uses pictures or symbols to show data.

Favorite Colors

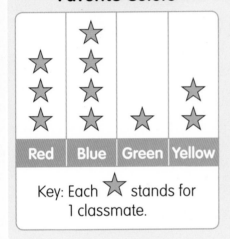

| Red | Blue | Green | Yellow |

Key: Each ★ stands for 1 classmate.

Bar Graphs

A bar graph uses a scale and bars to show data.

a vertical bar graph

Flowers on Four Plants

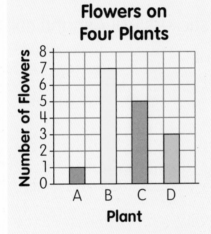

b horizontal bar graph

Animals on a Farm

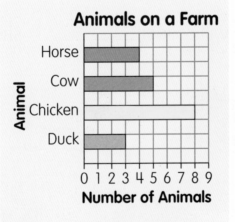

Line Plots

A line plot shows data on a number line.

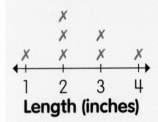

Length (inches)

Key: Each ✗ stands for 1 leaf.

Name: _____   Date: _____

Look at the picture graph.
Then, fill in each blank.

The picture graph shows the amount of money Carson earned during his summer vacation.

Amount of Money Carson Earned

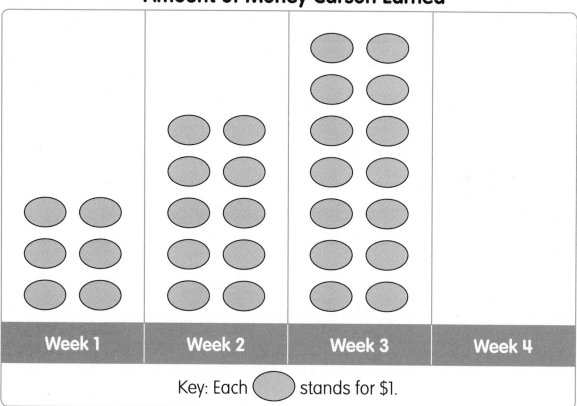

Key: Each ⬭ stands for $1.

1. Carson earned $22 in Week 3 and Week 4.
   Complete the picture graph for Week 4.

2. The total amount of money Carson earned in Week _____ and Week _____ is the same as the amount he earned in Week 3.

3. The amount of money Carson earned in Week 3 is $_____ less than the total amount of money he earned in Week 1 and Week 2.

4. Carson earned $_____ in all.

Complete the tally chart.

Sarah saw different types of birds on a road trip.
She recorded her data in a tally chart.

Type of Birds	Tally	Number of Birds
Jay	✝✝✝ ✝✝✝ ||	
Robin	✝✝✝ ✝✝✝ ✝✝✝	
Flamingo	✝✝✝ ✝✝✝ ||	
Peacock	✝✝✝ ||||	

Use the tally chart in ⑤ to complete the bar graph.
Then, give it a title.

⑥

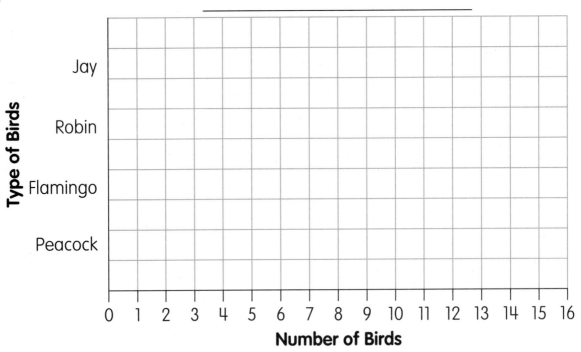

Look at the bar graph.
Then, fill in each blank.

A group of children went on a bug hunt.
The bar graph shows the number of bugs they found in different places.

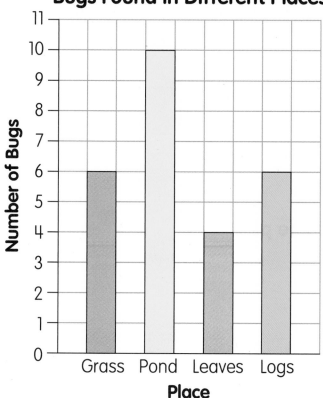

Bugs Found in Different Places

7 They found the same number of bugs on the _____ and
on the _____.

8 They found _____ bugs in the pond and on the leaves.

9 They found _____ bugs in all.

10 The total number of bugs they found in the pond and on the logs
is _____ more than the total number of bugs found on the
grass and on the leaves.

Mr. Wright measured the heights of a group of children. Then, he recorded the data in a chart.

Height (inches)				
53	49	50	56	57
49	53	49	53	57
52	54	53	54	54
50	51	50	49	56
57	52	49	53	49

Use the chart to complete the line plot.

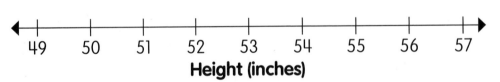

Height (inches)

Key: Each X stands for 1 child.

Assessment Prep

Complete the tally chart.

12 Tristan measured the length of some ribbons.
Then, he recorded the data in the tally chart below.

Length (inches)	Tally	Number of Ribbons
1					
2						
3					
4								

Use the tally chart to complete the bar graph.
Then, give it a title.

13

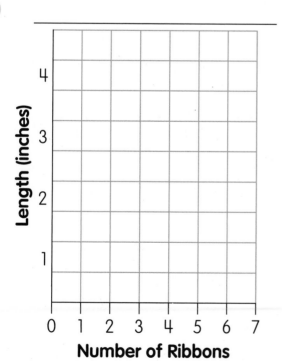

Complete the line plot to show the data on the previous page.

14

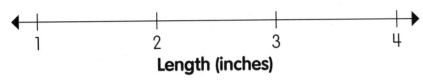

Length (inches)

Key: Each ✗ stands for 1 ribbon.

Make a ✗ in the box with the incorrect statements.

15 The number of ribbons with a length of 1 inch and 3 inches is the same.

☐

16 There are 6 ribbons with a length of 4 inches.

☐

17 There are 20 ribbons in all.

☐

18 There are 4 ribbons with at least a length of 2 inches.

☐

19 There are 7 ribbons with at most a length of 2 inches.

☐

20 There are 13 ribbons with a length of 3 inches or less.

☐

Name: _____ Date: _____

In an Eco Garden

The animals shown below are found near a pond.

1 Draw a picture graph.

Use △ to stand for 1 animal.

Animals Found Near a Pond

Snail	**Frog**	**Butterfly**	**Dragonfly**

Key: Each _____ stands for 1 animal.

2 How many animals are there in all? _____

3 Measure the length of some leaves found in a garden. Use the tally chart below to record your data.

Length (inches)	Tally	Number of Leaves

4 Draw a bar graph to show your data.

Lengths of Leaves

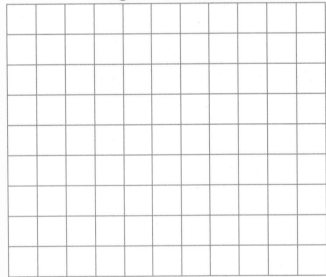

5 Draw a line plot to show your data.

6 Which way of representing data do you prefer? Why?

Rubric

Point(s)	Level	My Performance
7–8	4	• Most of my answers are correct. • I show all my work correctly. • I explain my thinking clearly and completely.
5–6.5	3	• Some of my answers are correct. • I show some of my work correctly. • I explain my thinking clearly.
3–4.5	2	• A few of my answers are correct. • I show little work correctly. • I explain some of my thinking clearly.
0–2.5	1	• A few of my answers are correct. • I show little or no work. • I do not explain my thinking clearly.

Teacher's Comments

What are the different ways to multiply and divide?

Name: _____ Date: _____

Adding equal groups

2 + 2 + 2 + 2 = 8
4 groups of 2 = 8
    4 twos = 8

▶ **Quick Check**

Fill in each blank.

1

_____ groups of _____ = _____

2 4 threes = _____ + _____ + _____ + _____ = _____

3 5 fours = _____ groups of _____ = _____

Circle the set that does not belong.

4 [14] [4 + 7 + 4 + 7] [2 groups of 7] [7 + 7]

5 [8 + 8 + 8 + 8 + 8] [5 groups of 8] [8 + 5] [5 eights]

How to Multiply

Learning Objectives:
- Use equal groups and repeated addition to multiply.
- Make multiplication sentences.

New Vocabulary
equal groups
multiply
repeated addition
times
multiplication sentence

 **THINK**

Kevin has two long pieces of wood.
On the first day, he cuts each piece of wood into two equal pieces.
He continues to cut each piece of wood into two equal pieces every day.
How many pieces of wood will he have after 4 days?

What information do I know?
What do I need to find out?

ENGAGE

Take some .

How many  are there in all?

Explain and show how you find the answer in two or more ways.

LEARN Use equal groups to multiply

1 How many toy bears are there?

> You can use repeated addition or multiplication to find the number of toy bears.

a There are 2 groups.
Each group has 6 toy bears.

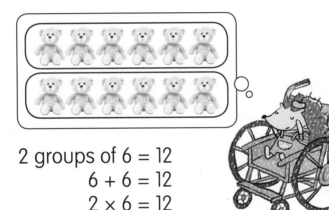

2 groups of 6 = 12
6 + 6 = 12
2 × 6 = 12

There are 12 toy bears in all.

> 2 sixes = 12
> '2 × 6' is the same as 12.

> × is read as times.
> It means to multiply or to put all the equal groups together.

2 × 6 = 12 is a **multiplication sentence**.
You read it as two times six equals twelve.

b There are 6 groups.
Each group has 2 toy bears.

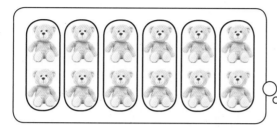

6 groups of 2 = 12
2 + 2 + 2 + 2 + 2 + 2 = 12
6 × 2 = 12

There are 12 toy bears
in all.

6 twos = 12
'6 × 2' is the same as 12.

'2 × 6' is the same as '6 × 2'.
2 × 6 = 6 × 2

2 Multiply 5 by 2.

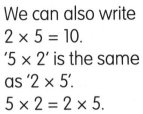

First, count the number of eggs in each nest.
There are 5 eggs in each nest.

Then, count the number of nests.
There are 2 nests.

$5 \times 2 = 10$
There are 10 eggs in all.

We can also write
$2 \times 5 = 10$.
'5×2' is the same
as '2×5'.
$5 \times 2 = 2 \times 5$.

Hands-on Activity Order of multiplication

Work in small groups.

① Use to show 2×3.

② Ask your classmate to use to show 3×2.

③ Use repeated addition to find the answer.
Then, compare the answers in ① and ②.

④ Repeat ① to ③ with these.

   a 5×6 and 6×5 b 7×10 and 10×7

⑤ Share what you notice with your classmates.

© 2020 Marshall Cavendish Education Pte Ltd

TRY Practice using equal groups to multiply

Fill in each blank.

1 How many candles are there in all?

5 groups of 2 = _____

2 + 2 + 2 + 2 + 2 = _____

5 × 2 = _____

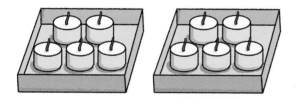

2 groups of 5 = _____

5 + 5 = _____

2 × 5 = _____

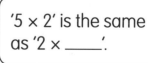
'5 × 2' is the same as '2 × ____'.

2 How many hair clips are there in all?

3 + 3 + 3 + 3 = _____

4 × _____ = _____

There are _____ hair clips in all.

_____ + _____ + _____ = _____

_____ × _____ = _____

There are _____ hair clips in all.

'4 × _____' is the same as '3 × _____'.

Multiply.
Fill in each blank.

3 Multiply 3 by 5.

_____ × _____ = _____

There are _____ muffins in all.

You can use repeated addition to help you find the answer.

4 Multiply 6 by 4.

_____ × _____ = _____

There are _____ cherries in all.

5 Multiply 7 by 3.

_____ × _____ = _____

There are _____ carrots in all.

MATCH THEM!

What you need:

Players: 3
Materials: Multiplication cards

What to do:

1 Shuffle the cards.
Give ten cards to each player and put the rest of the stack in the middle of the playing area.

2 Draw a card from the stack.
If a match is found, put the pair of cards in front of you.
If no match is found, return the card to the bottom of the stack.

3 Take turns. Repeat **2**.

Example

2×4 is the same as 4×2.

Put the pair of cards in front of you.

2×4 is not the same as 4×3.

Who is the winner?

The first player who matches all the cards wins the game.

Name: _____   Date: _____

INDEPENDENT PRACTICE

Look at the pictures.
Fill in each blank.

1

4 groups of 5 monkeys = _____

5 + 5 + 5 + 5 = _____

4 × 5 = _____

5 groups of 4 monkeys = _____

4 + 4 + 4 + 4 + 4 = _____

5 × 4 = _____

'4 × ____' is the same as '5 × ____'.

2

6 threes = _____

3 + 3 + 3 + 3 + 3 + 3 = _____

6 × 3 = _____

3 sixes = _____

6 + 6 + 6 = _____

3 × 6 = _____

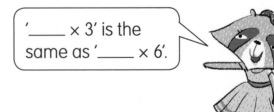

'_____ × 3' is the same as '_____ × 6'.

Fill in each blank.

3

2 + 2 + 2 = _____

3 × _____ = _____

3 + 3 = _____

2 × _____ = _____

4

_____ + _____ + _____ + _____ + _____ = _____

_____ × _____ = _____

_____ + _____ + _____ + _____ + _____ + _____ + _____ = _____

_____ × _____ = _____

Multiply.
Fill in each blank.

5 Multiply 2 by 5.

_____ × _____ = _____

6 Multiply 10 by 4.

_____ × _____ = _____

7 Multiply 8 by 3.

_____ × _____ = _____

2 How to Divide

Learning Objectives:
- Use objects or pictures to find the number of items in each group when sharing equally.
- Use objects or pictures to find the number of equal groups.
- Relate repeated subtraction to division.
- Make division sentences.

New Vocabulary
share equally
repeated subtraction
divide
division sentence

 **THINK**

Daniela bakes 10 cookies.
She wants to give 4 friends the same number of cookies.
She realises that there are not enough cookies.
How many more cookies does she need?
What is the fewest number of cookies Daniela still needs?

What information do I know?
What do I need to find out?
What can I do first?

ENGAGE

Take 6 🎲 to give to 2 classmates.
Each classmate receives the same number of 🎲.
Make a story to show what you did.

1 Callia has 6 muffins.
She has 3 friends.
She gives each friend the same number of muffins in a bag.

Callia puts 1 muffin into each bag.
She has 3 muffins left.

Then, she puts 1 more muffin into each bag.
Now she has no muffins left.

Each friend gets 2 muffins.

Math Talk

Can Mark give 6 muffins equally to 4 friends? Why?
Use to explain to your partner.

Hands-on Activity Sharing equally

Work in pairs.

1 Take 20 and 4 paper plates.

2 Put all the equally on each plate.

3 How many are there on each plate?

4 Repeat 1 to 3 with these.

  a 24   b 32

TRY Practice sharing equally

Fill in the blank.

1 Gabriel has to put 8 pots equally on 4 racks.

He puts 1 pot on each rack.

Then, he puts 1 more pot on each rack.

Each rack has _____ pots.

Draw.
Then, fill in each blank.

2 Damian has to put 10 flowers equally into 2 groups.
Help Damian put the rest of the flowers equally in each group.

Each group has _____ flowers.

3 Aiden has to put 15 balls equally into 5 groups.
Help Aiden put the rest of the balls equally in each group.

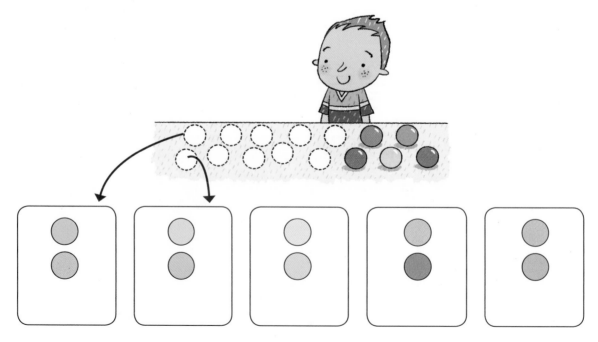

Each group has _____ balls.

ENGAGE

a Put 9 pencils on a table.
If each student takes 3 pencils, how many students are there?

b There are some pencils on another table.
The same group of students each takes 3 pencils.
There are some pencils left.
What is a possible number of pencils on the table at first?

LEARN Find the number of equal groups

1. There are 12 eggs.
Put 4 eggs into each bowl.
How many bowls do I need?

First, put 4 eggs into 1 bowl.

Do this until all the eggs are put into the bowls.

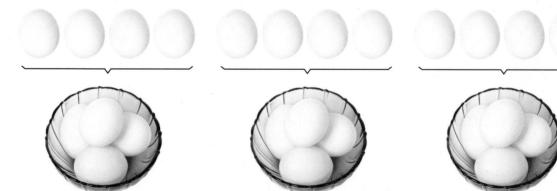

I need 3 bowls.
There are 3 equal groups.

Hands-on Activity Finding the number of equal groups

Work in pairs.

① Take 20 ● and some cups.

② Put 2 ● in each cup.

③ How many cups do you use?

④ Repeat ① to ③ with these.

   a   Put 4 ● in each cup.

   b   Put 5 ● in each cup.

   c   Put 10 ● in each cup.

What multiplication sentence can you think of?

TRY Practice finding the number of equal groups

Circle.
Then, fill in each blank.

① There are 16 butterflies.
Circle groups of 4.

There are _____ groups of 4 butterflies.

② There are 20 apples.
Circle groups of 5.

There are _____ groups of 5 apples.

ENGAGE

There are 8 .

a Take 2  at a time until there are no  left.
How many times did you take the ?

b Take 3 .
Are there any 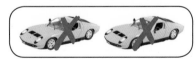 left?
What other number of 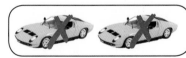 can you use in **a**?

LEARN Use repeated subtraction to divide

1 Irene has 6 toy cars.
She wants to give 2 toy cars to each of her friends.
How many friends receive toy cars from her?

First, she gives 2 toy cars to Orion.
How many toy cars does she have left?

$6 - 2 = 4$
She has 4 toy cars left.

Then, she gives 2 toy cars to June.
How many toy cars does she have left?

$4 - 2 = 2$
She has 2 toy cars left.

Finally, she gives 2 toy cars to Noah.
How many toy cars does she have left?

2 − 2 = 0
She has 0 toy cars left.

Subtract 2 until you get 0.
How many times do you
subtract 2?

3 times!

Irene divides her 6 toy cars equally by giving
2 toy cars to each friend.
So, 3 friends receive toy cars from her.

6 − 2 − 2 − 2 = 0 is the same as 6 ÷ 2 = 3.

Groups of 2 are subtracted 3 times.
This is repeated subtraction.

÷ is read as divided by.
÷ stands for division.

6 ÷ 2 = 3 is a division sentence.
You read it as six divided by two equals three.

2 Divide 9 by 3.

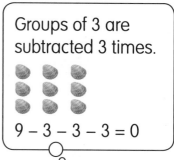

Groups of 3 are subtracted 3 times.

$9 - 3 - 3 - 3 = 0$

$9 \div 3 = 3$
There are 3 groups of 3 seashells.

Hands-on Activity Dividing equally

Work in pairs.

① Take some  to show 'Divide 12 by 4' in two ways.

② Write division sentences to show the division.

Example:

i

$12 \div 4 = 3$
I divide 12 cubes equally into 4 groups.
Each group has 3 cubes.

ii

$12 \div 4 = 3$
I divide 12 cubes in groups of 4.
There are 3 groups.

(3) Trade places.

Repeat (1) and (2) for the following.

a   Divide 20 by 4.

i   _____ ÷ _____ = _____   ii   _____ ÷ _____ = _____

I divide _____ cubes   I divide _____ cubes into

equally into _____ groups.   groups of _____.

Each group has _____ cubes.   There are _____ groups.

b   Divide 24 by 3.

i   _____ ÷ _____ = _____   ii   _____ ÷ _____ = _____

I divide _____ cubes   I divide _____ cubes into

equally into _____ groups.   groups of _____.

Each group has _____ cubes.   There are _____ groups.

TRY Practice using repeated subtraction to divide

Fill in each blank.

(1) Put 12 books into stacks of 2.

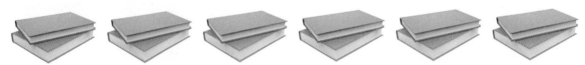

12 – 2 – 2 – 2 – 2 – 2 – 2 = _____

12 ÷ 2 = _____

There are _____ stacks of books.

2 Put 15 stickers into groups of 5.

15 – _____ – _____ – _____ = _____

15 ÷ _____ = _____

There are _____ groups of 5 stickers.

3 Divide 18 by 3.

18 – _____ – _____ – _____ – _____ – _____ = _____

_____ ÷ _____ = _____

There are _____ children with 3 oranges.

4 Divide 20 by 4.

20 – _____ – _____ – _____ – _____ – _____ = _____

_____ ÷ _____ = _____

There are _____ groups of clips.

Divide.
Fill in each blank.

5 Put 16 cherries equally into 8 groups.

_____ ÷ _____ = _____

There are _____ cherries in each group.

6 Divide 14 cups into groups of 7.

_____ ÷ _____ = _____

There are _____ groups of 7 cups.

7 Divide 18 erasers equally into 2 groups.

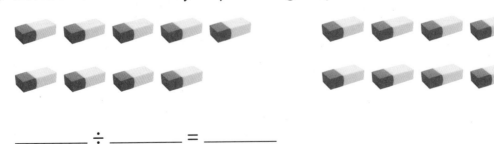

_____ ÷ _____ = _____

There are _____ erasers in each group.

INDEPENDENT PRACTICE

Draw.
Then, fill in each blank.

1 There are 12 apples.
Kimberly puts them equally into 2 bags.
Draw an equal number of apples in each bag.

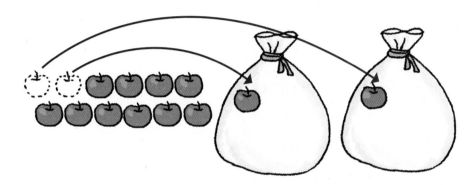

There are _____ apples in each bag.

2 There are 16 buttons.
They are shared equally by 4 children.
In each bag, draw an equal number of buttons for each child.

Each child gets _____ buttons.

Fill in each blank.

3 Put 21 paper clips into 3 equal groups.

There are _____ paper clips in each group.

4 Put 24 triangles into 4 equal groups.

There are _____ triangles in each group.

5 Put 20 crayons into 5 equal groups.

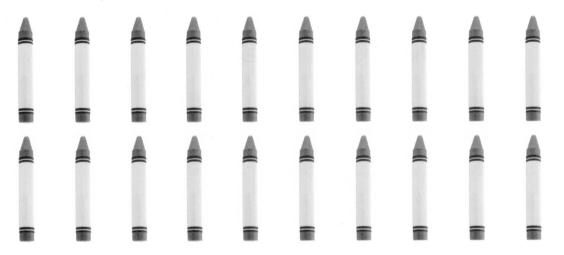

There are _____ crayons in each group.

Circle.
Then, fill in each blank.

6 There are 10 beanies.
Circle groups of 2.

There are _____ groups of _____ beanies.

7 12 children go skating.
Circle groups of 6.

There are _____ groups of _____ children.

8 There are 15 oranges.

Circle groups of _____ oranges.

There are _____ groups of _____ oranges.

9 There are 14 trucks.

Circle groups of _____ trucks.

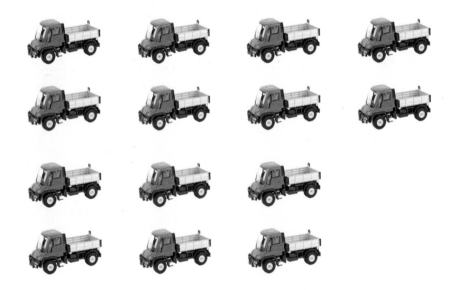

There are _____ groups of _____ trucks.

Fill in each blank.

10 Put 10 caps into groups of 5.

$10 - 5 - 5 =$ _____

_____ $\div$ _____ $=$ _____

There are _____ groups of 5 caps.

11 Put 15 pancakes onto plates of 3.

_____ $-$ _____ $-$ _____ $-$ _____ $-$ _____ $-$ _____ $=$ _____

_____ $\div$ _____ $=$ _____

There are _____ plates of 3 pancakes.

12 Divide 12 beads into groups of 4.

_____ $-$ _____ $-$ _____ $-$ _____ $=$ _____

_____ $\div$ _____ $=$ _____

There are _____ groups of 4 beads.

13 Divide 16 by 4.

_____ – _____ – _____ – _____ – _____ = _____

_____ ÷ _____ = _____

There are _____ children each with 4 balloons.

14 Divide 20 by 10.

_____ – _____ – _____ = _____

_____ ÷ _____ = _____

There are _____ bundles of 10 pencils.

Divide.
Fill in each blank.

15 Divide 9 by 3.

_____ ÷ _____ = _____

There are _____ eggs in each nest.

16 Arrange 16 books equally into 4 stacks.

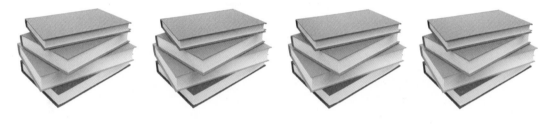

_____ ÷ _____ = _____

There are _____ books in each stack.

17 Divide 10 snails equally into 2 groups.

_____ ÷ _____ = _____

There are _____ snails in each group.

18 Divide 14 leaves into groups of 7.

_____ ÷ _____ = _____

There are _____ groups of 7 leaves.

19 Divide 20 by 5.

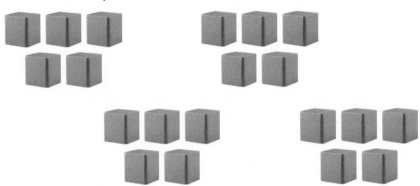

_____ ÷ _____ = _____

There are _____ groups of 5 cubes.

20 Divide 15 hats into groups of 3.

_____ ÷ _____ = _____

There are _____ groups of 3 hats.

3 Real-World Problems: Multiplication and Division

Learning Objective:
- Solve real-world problems involving multiplication and division.

THINK

Liam is thinking of a month in the calendar.
There are 7 days in a week.
There are exactly 4 weeks in the month.
Which month is he thinking about?

ENGAGE

Use  to show these facts.
Then, find each answer.

a 5×4 **b** 4×5

What do you notice?
Make a story to show what you did.

LEARN Solve real-world problems involving multiplication and division

1. There are 3 children.
   The teacher gives each child 6 stickers.
   How many stickers does the teacher give in all?

$3 \times 6 = 18$
The teacher gives 18 stickers in all.

2 Ms. Gray has 14 markers.
She divides them equally among 7 children.
How many markers does each child receive?

$14 \div 7 = 2$
Each child receives 2 markers.

3 Some children collect 24 seashells.
Each child collects 4 seashells.
How many children are there in all?

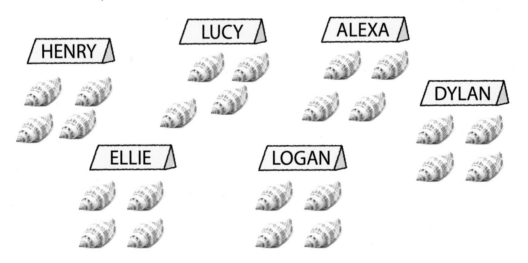

HENRY   LUCY   ALEXA   DYLAN   ELLIE   LOGAN

$24 \div 4 = 6$
There are 6 children in all.

Work in groups.

1. Use the picture above to make some multiplication and division stories about:

   a   balloons   b   sandwiches   c   drinks

2. Write multiplication and division sentences for each story.

   Example:

   5 children have 2 hats each.
   There are 10 hats in all.
   5 × 2 = 10
   10 ÷ 5 = 2

   Your story:

   Multiplication and division sentences:

TRY Practice solving real-world problems involving multiplication and division

Fill in each blank.

1. Karina has 2 pencil cases.
There are 4 erasers in each pencil case.
How many erasers does she have in all?

_____ × _____ = _____

She has _____ erasers in all.

2. Mr. Patel puts 7 books on each row of a bookcase.
How many books does he have in all?

_____ × _____ = _____

He has _____ books in all.

3 A clown has 18 balloons.
He gives an equal number of balloons to 9 children.
How many balloons does each child receive?

_____ ÷ _____ = _____

Each child receives _____ balloons.

4 Ms. Myers bakes 16 apple tarts.
She wants to put 8 apple tarts in each box.
How many boxes does she need?

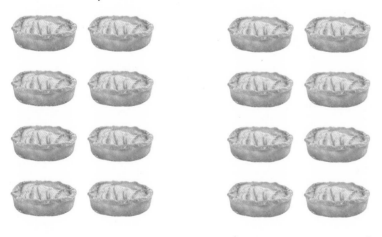

_____ ÷ _____ = _____

She needs _____ boxes.

WRITE AND SOLVE!

What you need:

Players: 2
Materials: Multiplication cards, Division cards

What to do:

1. Shuffle the cards. Then, draw a card.

2. Write a multiplication or a division real-world problem using the card.

3. Have your partner solve the real-world problem.

4. Check the answer.

5. Trade roles. Repeat 1 to 4.

Who is the winner?

The player with the most correct answers after 5 rounds wins!

INDEPENDENT PRACTICE

Fill in each blank.

1. Ryan has 4 jars.
There are 6 biscuits in each jar.
How many biscuits does he have in all?

_____ × _____ = _____

He has _____ biscuits in all.

2. Lilian has 5 boxes.
There are 8 pencils in each box.
How many pencils does she have in all?

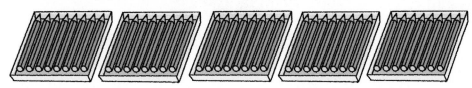

_____ × _____ = _____

She has _____ pencils in all.

3 Mr. Brooks buys 18 kites.
   He gives an equal number of kites to his 6 nephews.
   How many kites does each of his nephews receive?

   _____ ÷ _____ = _____

   Each nephew receives _____ kites.

4 Ms. Long has 28 tomatoes.
   She puts 7 tomatoes in each basket.
   How many baskets does she have?

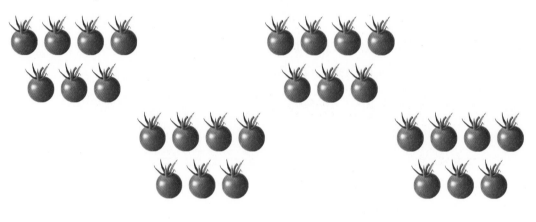

   _____ ÷ _____ = _____

   She has _____ baskets.

5 Hailey has 9 dresses.
   There are 2 buttons on each dress.
   How many buttons are there in all?

Do you multiply
or divide?

4 Odd and Even Numbers

Learning Objectives:
• Make groups of 2 to find odd and even numbers.
• Understand that an even number is the sum of two equal numbers.

New Vocabulary
odd number
even number

 **THINK**

Take 10 counters.
Divide them equally into 2 groups.
How many are left over?
Now, divide the 10 counters into 3 equal groups.
Do you have any left over?
Will you always have left over counters when you divide any number of counters by 3?

ENGAGE

Yong has 20 forks and spoons in all.
How many pairs of a fork and a spoon can he make?
Use  to show your answer.
Share your thinking with your partner.

LEARN Make groups of 2 to find odd and even numbers

1 Put 5 apples into groups of 2.

There is 1 apple left.
5 is an odd number .

2 Put 6 pears into groups of 2.

There are no pears left.
6 is an even number .

3 4 is an even number.

$$4 = 2 + 2$$

When you add two numbers that are the same, you will always get an even number.

4 10 is an even number.

$$10 = 5 + 5$$

Math Talk

Tell your partner why 8 is an even number and 11 is an odd number.

Hands-on Activity Recognizing even and odd numbers

1 Take 7 .
Group them in this way.

Do you have an even or odd number of cubes?
Why?

_____

② Gather 10 .
Stack them in groups of 2.
Is 10 an even or odd number? _____

③ Gather 12 .
Stack them in groups of 2.
Is 12 an even or odd number? _____

④ Gather 15 .
Stack them in groups of 2.
Is 15 an even or odd number? _____

⑤ How do you know that the number of cubes is even?

_____

⑥ How do you know that the number of cubes is odd?

_____

TRY Practice making groups of 2 to find odd and even numbers

Circle to make groups of 2.
Then, answer each question.

① There are 16 triangles in all.

Is 16 an even or odd number? _____

2 There are 13 stars in all.

★ ★ ★ ★ ★ ★ ★

★ ★ ★ ★ ★ ★

Is 13 an even or odd number? _____

Fill in each blank.

3 $6 = 3 +$ _____

4 $14 =$ _____ $+ 7$

5 _____ $= 9 + 9$

 **Math Talk**

3, 5, and 7 are odd numbers.
I cannot group them in twos.
But when I add them, the result is even.

You are right!
$3 + 5 = 8$, 8 is an even number.
$5 + 7 = 12$, 12 is an even number.
$3 + 7 = 10$, 10 is an even number.

Use some ⚪⚪ to show why is this so.
Find out if it is true when you add an odd number and an even number.

Name: _____   Date: _____

INDEPENDENT PRACTICE

Circle to make groups of 2.
Answer each question.
Then, fill in each blank with odd or even.

1

Are there any 🐘 left? _____

How many left? _____

11 is an _____ number.

2

Are there any 🍑 left? _____

How many left? _____

20 is an _____ number.

Draw.
Circle to make groups of 2.
Then, fill in each blank with odd or even.

3 Draw 26 ♥.

26 is an _____ number.

4 Draw 19 ✿.

19 is an _____ number.

Fill in each blank.
Use numbers that are the same.

5 8 = 4 + _____

6 12 = _____ + 6

7 10 = _____ + _____

8 22 = _____ + _____

Mathematical Habit 3 Construct viable arguments

Put 12 stars into equal groups in different ways.
What are the multiplication sentences and division sentences that you can write?
Draw circles around the stars to help you.

★ ★ ★ ★ ★ ★ ★ ★ ★ ★ ★ ★

Problem Solving with Heuristics

1 **Mathematical Habit** **8** **Look for patterns**

Faith is making silly toy animals.
Study the number of eyes each toy animal has.
Find a pattern.
Then, draw the eyes Faith will put on the last two toy animals.

2 **Mathematical Habit 1** **Persevere in solving problems**

Luke and Audrey have the same number of bowls.
They have 21 strawberries in all.
How many strawberries does Luke have?

I have 5 strawberries in each bowl.

I have 2 strawberries in each bowl.

I can solve this problem by making a list.

? What are the different ways to multiply and divide?

Multiplication and Division

Multiplication

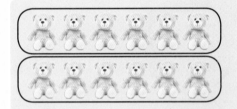

$6 + 6 = 12$
$2 \times 6 = 12$

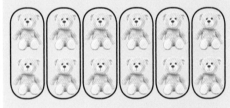

$2 + 2 + 2 + 2 + 2 + 2 = 12$
$6 \times 2 = 12$
$2 \times 6 = 6 \times 2$

Division

a sharing equally

$6 \div 3 = 2$

b finding equal groups

$12 - 4 - 4 - 4 = 0$
$12 \div 4 = 3$

Solving Real-World Problems

a There are 3 students.
The teacher gives each student 6 stickers.
How many stickers does the teacher give in all?
$3 \times 6 = 18$
The teacher gives 18 stickers in all.

b Ms. Reed has 14 markers.
She divides them equally among 7 children.
How many markers does each child get?
$14 \div 7 = 2$
Each child gets 2 markers.

Odd and Even Numbers

a odd number

There is 1 apple left.
5 in an odd number.

b even number

There are no pears left.
6 is an even number.

Name: _____ Date: _____

Write +, −, ×, or ÷.

1 6 groups of 2 = 6 ◯ 2

2 8 ◯ 4 = 32

3 3 × 5 = 5 ◯ 5 ◯ 5

4 20 ◯ 4 ◯ 4 ◯ 4 ◯ 4 ◯ 4 = 0

5 20 ◯ 5 = 4

6 15 ◯ 3 = 5

Fill in each blank.

7

4 × 3 = _____

There are _____ bees on the flowers in all.

8 Place 8 bananas onto 4 plates equally.

$8 \div 4 =$ _____

There are _____ bananas on each plate.

Solve.

9 Every day, Mr. Morgan collects 3 eggs from his hens. How many eggs does he collect in a week?

10 Claire has 35 stickers.
She puts 7 stickers on each page.
How many pages does she use?

Draw.
Circle to make groups of 2.
Then, fill in the blank.

11 Draw 17 triangles.

17 is an _____ number.

Fill in each blank.
Use numbers that are the same.

12 $2 = 1 +$ _____

13 $4 = 2 +$ _____

14 $16 =$ _____ $+$ _____

15 $20 =$ _____ $+$ _____

Assessment Prep

Answer each question.

16 How many rabbits are there in all?
Put a ✗ on the boxes with the incorrect answers.

5 groups of 2   5 + 5 + 5 + 5 + 5

2 + 2 + 2 + 2 + 2   5 × 2

5 + 5

17 How many groups of ducklings are there?
Put a ✗ on the boxes with the incorrect answers.

30 + 5   30 ÷ 6   30 − 6 − 6 − 6 − 6 − 6

5 × 6   30 ÷ 5

30 − 5 − 5 − 5 − 5 − 5 − 5

Name: _____   Date: _____

At the Sports Store

1 Use repeated addition to find the answer.

$3 \times 4 =$ _____

Color the dots to match the addition sentence.

2 Jackson gave away 4 gifts to his friends.
There were 6 bean bags in each gift.
How many bean bags did he give away in all?

3 Kylie used a number pattern to help her arrange the balls.
Find the number pattern.
Draw the fourth pattern.

1st   2nd   3rd   4th

How did you find the pattern?

4 Look at the picture.
Fill in the missing numbers.

☐ × ☐ = ☐

☐ ÷ ☐ = ☐

5 Divide 32 tennis balls equally into 4 boxes.
How many tennis balls are there in each box?

© 2020 Marshall Cavendish Education Pte Ltd

Rubric

Point(s)	Level	My Performance
7–8	4	• Most of my answers are correct. • I show all my work correctly. • I explain my thinking clearly and completely.
5–6	3	• Some of my answers are correct. • I show some of my work correctly. • I explain my thinking clearly.
3–4	2	• A few of my answers are correct. • I show little work correctly. • I explain some of my thinking clearly.
0–2	1	• A few of my answers are correct. • I show little or no work. • I do not explain my thinking clearly.

Teacher's Comments

STEAM

House Sparrows

Have you seen small brown birds near your home or school?
They may be House Sparrows [SPARE-ohz].
They arrived in New York in 1851.
Since then, they have spread across the country.
The birds hop on the ground, looking for seeds.
They also catch insects and visit bird feeders.

Task

Feed the Birds

Work in 10 pairs.

1. As a class, pour three piles of these bird foods:
   • sunflower seeds • corn • white millet

2. Work together to divide each pile into 10 equal groups.

3. Take one group of each type of bird food for you and your partner.

4. Mix the food together on a paper plate.

5. Use a plastic knife to spread honey or peanut butter on an empty toilet paper roll. Stick the food to the roll.

6. Pull a long piece of string through the roll. Tie the string on one end.

7. Hang your bird feeder outside. Count the number of birds feeding on it. Use the number you count and multiplication to predict how many birds will visit the feeder in one school week.

2 toy soldiers walking in a line,
2 toy soldiers walking in a line,
If 2 more soldiers join them in the line,
There will be 4 toy soldiers walking in a line.

4 toy soldiers walking in a line,
4 toy soldiers walking in a line,
If 2 more soldiers join them in the line,
There will be 6 toy soldiers walking in a line.

6 toy soldiers walking in a line,
6 toy soldiers walking in a line,
If 2 more soldiers join them in the line,
There will be 8 toy soldiers walking in a line.

How can you use known multiplication facts to find other multiplication facts?

Finding numbers in patterns

a   2, 4, 6, 8, 10, 12, 14, 16, 18, 20

b   5, 10, 15, 20, 25, 30, 35, 40, 45, 50

c   10, 20, 30, 40, 50, 60, 70, 80, 90, 100

▶ **Quick Check**

Find each missing number.

1 2, 4, 6, 8, 10, _____, _____, _____, _____

2 5, 10, 15, 20, _____, _____, _____, _____, _____

3 _____, _____, _____, _____, 60, 50, 40, 30

Using equal groups to multiply

a

b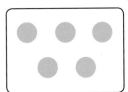

5 groups of 2 = 10
5 twos = 10
2 + 2 + 2 + 2 + 2 = 10
5 × 2 = 10

2 groups of 5 = 10
2 fives = 10
5 + 5 = 10
2 × 5 = 10

▶ **Quick Check**

Fill in each blank.

  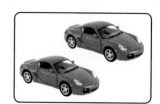

_____ groups of 2 = _____

_____ twos = _____

_____ + _____ + _____ + _____ + _____ + _____ = _____

_____ × _____ = _____

_____ groups of 5 = _____

_____ fives = _____

_____ + _____ + _____ + _____ = _____

_____ × _____ = _____

RECALL PRIOR KNOWLEDGE

6

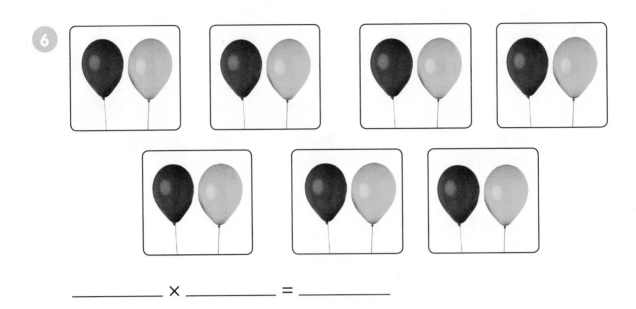

_____ × _____ = _____

7

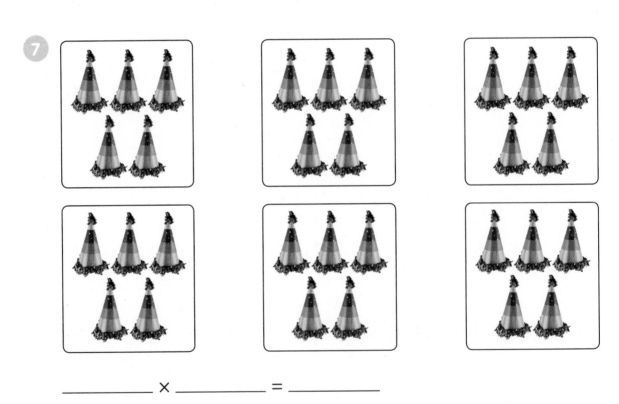

_____ × _____ = _____

Multiplying by 2

Learning Objectives:
- Skip count by 2s.
- Use known multiplication facts to find other multiplication facts.

New Vocabulary
skip count
dot paper

THINK

a   Recall using repeated addition to multiply.
How do you use repeated addition to find 8×2?
How can you find the answer in two different ways?
Share with your partner how you find the answer.

b   How can you use multiplication table of 2 to show 18?
Explain and show how you find out.

ENGAGE

Use ⬤ to show 4×2.
Take 2 more ⬤.
How many ⬤ do you have in all?
Write a multiplication sentence to show your answer.

Hands-on Activity ▸ Doubling a number

Work in pairs.

① Take some 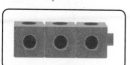 to show 'double 3' to your partner.

② Write two equations to show 'double 3'.

Example:

$2 \times 3 = 6$
$3 + 3 = 6$

(3) Trade places. Repeat ① and ② for the following.

a Double 4

_____ × _____ = _____

_____ + _____ = _____

b Double 5

_____ × _____ = _____

_____ + _____ = _____

LEARN Skip count by 2s

① $1 \times 2 = 2$

 $2 + 2 = 4$
$2 \times 2 = 4$

 $4 + 2 = 6$
$3 \times 2 = 6$

$6 + 2 = 8$
$4 \times 2 = 8$

 $8 + 2 = 10$
$5 \times 2 = 10$

 $10 + 2 = 12$
$6 \times 2 = 12$

$12 + 2 = 14$
$7 \times 2 = 14$

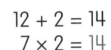 $14 + 2 = 16$
$8 \times 2 = 16$

$16 + 2 = 18$
$9 \times 2 = 18$

 $18 + 2 = 20$
$10 \times 2 = 20$

 I can skip count by adding 2 to get the next number.

2, 4, 6, 8, 10, 12, 14, 16, 18, 20

I count by 2s.

Math Talk
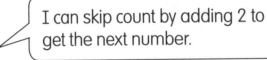
Jack uses double facts to find 2×2.
Tell your partner how to use double facts to find 2×2.

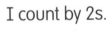

© 2020 Marshall Cavendish Education Pte Ltd

2 There are 4 trays.
Each tray has 2 glasses of juice.

4 groups of 2 glasses
4 × 2 = 8

There are 8 glasses
of juice.

This is a **dot paper**.
It shows 4 rows of 2.

3 Blake has 7 bags.
There are 2 pineapples in each bag.

7 groups of 2 pineapples
7 × 2 = 14

He has 14 pineapples in all.

 **Math Talk**

There are 8 pencil cases.
There are 2 erasers in each pencil case.
How many erasers are there in all?
Show your partner how you find
your answer.

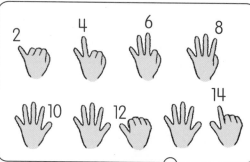

TRY Practice skip counting by 2s

Fill in each blank.

1

Find 2 groups of 2.

$2 \times 2 =$ _____

I can skip count by adding 2.

$+2$

2   4

2

Find 5 groups of 2.

$5 \times 2 =$ _____

3

Find 8 groups of 2.

$8 \times 2 =$ _____

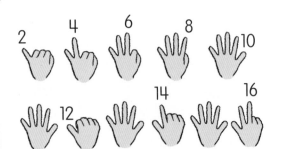

ENGAGE

Take 5 groups of 2 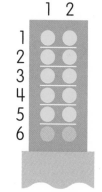.

How many more 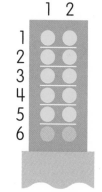 do you need to make 7 groups of 2 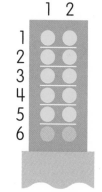?

How many 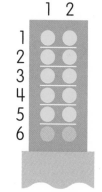 do you need to take away to make 4 groups of 2 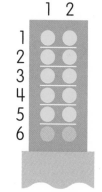?
Explain and show how you get your answers.

LEARN Use known multiplication facts to find other multiplication facts

1. $6 \times 2 = ?$

Start with 5 groups of 2.

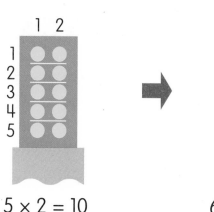

$5 \times 2 = 10$

$6 \times 2 = 10 + 2$
$= 12$

6 groups of 2 =
5 groups of 2 +
1 group of 2

6

5   1

Math Talk

Can you find 7×2 from 5×2?
Show your partner how you do it.
Use the dot paper to help you.

2 $9 \times 2 = ?$

Start with 10 groups of 2.

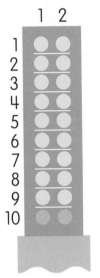

1 2

$10 \times 2 = 20$

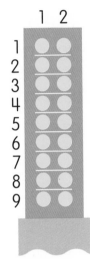

1 2

$9 \times 2 = 20 - 2$
$= 18$

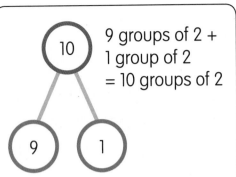

9 groups of 2 +
1 group of 2
= 10 groups of 2

So, 10 groups of 2 –
1 group of 2 =
9 groups of 2.

**Multiplication
Table of 2**

1	×	2	=	2
2	×	2	=	4
3	×	2	=	6
4	×	2	=	8
5	×	2	=	10
6	×	2	=	12
7	×	2	=	14
8	×	2	=	16
9	×	2	=	18
10	×	2	=	20

TRY Practice using known multiplication facts to find other multiplication facts

Find each missing number.
Use dot paper to help you.

1 $7 \times 2 = ?$

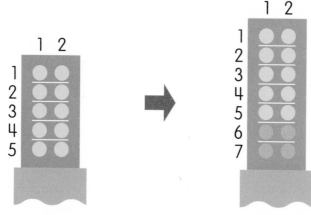

$5 \times 2 =$ _____

$7 \times 2 = 10 +$ _____

$=$ _____

2 $8 \times 2 = ?$

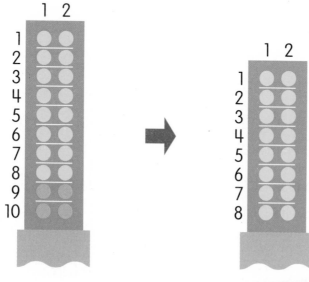

$10 \times 2 =$ _____

$8 \times 2 = 20 -$ _____

$=$ _____

THE TWOS!

What you need:

Players: 2
Materials: Multiplication by 2 cards

What to do:

Place the stack of multiplication cards face down.

1. Player 1 draws a multiplication card and answers the question. Player 2 checks the answer.

2. If player 1 gives the correct answer, he or she keeps the card. If not, Player 1 loses his or her turn.

3. Take turns to play. Do not return the cards to the stack after each turn.

Who is the winner?

The player with the most number of correct answers wins.

Name: _____   Date: _____

INDEPENDENT PRACTICE

Fill in each blank.
Use dot paper to help you.

Find 3 groups of 2.

3 × 2 = _____

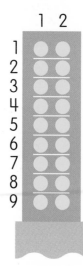

Find 6 groups of 2.

6 × 2 = _____

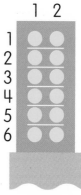

Find 9 groups of 2.

9 × 2 = _____

Skip count by 2s.
Then, fill in each blank.

4
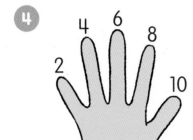

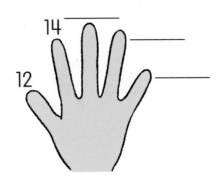

Fill in each blank.

5　6 × 2 = _____

6　3 × 2 = _____

7　7 × 2 = _____

8　4 × 2 = _____

9　9 × 2 = _____

10　5 × 2 = _____

11　8 × 2 = _____

12　1 × 2 = _____

13　10 × 2 = _____

14　2 × 2 = _____

Fill in each blank.
Use dot paper to help you.

15 4 × 2 = _____

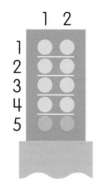 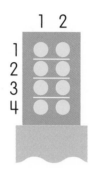

_____ × _____ = _____   4 × 2 = _____ − _____

                                            = _____

16 7 × 2 = _____

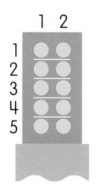 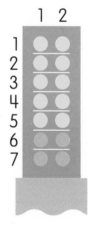

_____ × _____ = _____   7 × 2 = _____ + _____

                                            = _____

Color each shape.
Use the same color for the shapes that have the same value.

5 groups of 2

2 × 8

10

2 × 3

10 × 2

8

8 groups of 2

20

2 × 5

4 × 2

3 groups of 2

16

4 groups of 2

6 groups of 2

6 × 2

6

12

10 groups of 2

2 Multiplying by 5

Learning Objective:
• Skip count by 5s.

THINK

Recall using repeated addition to multiply.
How do you use repeated addition to find 7 × 5?
How can you find the answer in two different ways?
Share with your partner how you find the answer.

ENGAGE

Form 2 groups of 5 students.
Have another 5 students join the groups.
How many students are there in all?
Write a multiplication sentence to show your answer.

Hands-on Activity Skip counting by 5s using a hundreds chart

① Circle the number 5.

② Start from 5.
Skip count by 5 and circle the numbers.

1	2	3	4	5	6	7	8	9	10
11	12	13	14	15	16	17	18	19	20
21	22	23	24	25	26	27	28	29	30
31	32	33	34	35	36	37	38	39	40
41	42	43	44	45	46	47	48	49	50
51	52	53	54	55	56	57	58	59	60
61	62	63	64	65	66	67	68	69	70
71	72	73	74	75	76	77	78	79	80
81	82	83	84	85	86	87	88	89	90
91	92	93	94	95	96	97	98	99	100

③ What pattern do you notice?

Skip count by 5s

1

 $1 \times 5 = 5$

$5 + 5 = 10$
$2 \times 5 = 10$

$10 + 5 = 15$
$3 \times 5 = 15$

$15 + 5 = 20$
$4 \times 5 = 20$

$20 + 5 = 25$
$5 \times 5 = 25$

$25 + 5 = 30$
$6 \times 5 = 30$

$30 + 5 = 35$
$7 \times 5 = 35$

$35 + 5 = 40$
$8 \times 5 = 40$

$40 + 5 = 45$
$9 \times 5 = 45$

$45 + 5 = 50$
$10 \times 5 = 50$

> I can skip count by adding 5 to get the next number.

5, 10, 15, 20, 25, 30, 35, 40, 45, 50

 Math Talk

Find 5×5.
Show your partner how you find the answer.

> I count by 5s.

2 There are 2 bundles of balloons.
Each bundle has 5 balloons.

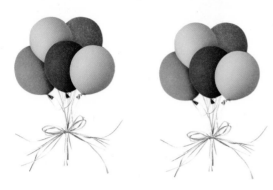

2 groups of 5 balloons
$2 \times 5 = 10$

There are 10 balloons in all.

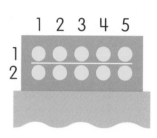

3 There are 3 groups of paintbrushes.
Each group has 5 paintbrushes.

3 groups of 5
paintbrushes
$3 \times 5 = 15$
There are 15
paintbrushes.

1 finger
stands for 5.

2 fingers
stand for 10.

3 fingers
stand for
$10 + 5 = 15$.

 **Math Talk**

Show your classmates how you use your
fingers to find 5×5 and 9×5.

Multiplication Table of 5

1	×	5	=	5
2	×	5	=	10
3	×	5	=	15
4	×	5	=	20
5	×	5	=	25
6	×	5	=	30
7	×	5	=	35
8	×	5	=	40
9	×	5	=	45
10	×	5	=	50

TRY Practice skip counting by 5s

Fill in each blank.

I can skip count by adding 5.

$$+5 \quad +5 \quad +5$$
$$5 \quad 10 \quad 15 \quad 20$$

Find 4 groups of 5.

4 × 5 = _____

2

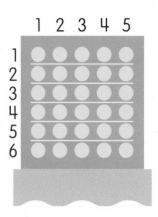

Find 6 groups of 5.

$6 \times 5 =$ _____

3

Find 7 groups of 5.

$7 \times 5 =$ _____

SPIN AND MULTIPLY!

What you need:

Players: 4–6
Materials: Multiplication spin card, Pencil

What to do:

Each player receives a multiplication spin card.

1. Place a pencil at the center of the multiplication spin card.

2. Player 1 spins the pencil.

3. The pencil points towards a number.
   Player 1 multiplies the number by 5 and writes the answer on the card.

4. The other players check the answer.

5. Player 1 gets a point if the answer is correct.

6. Trade places. Repeat 1 to 5.

Who is the winner?

The player with the most points after 8 rounds wins.

Name: _____ Date: _____

INDEPENDENT PRACTICE

Fill in each blank.
Use dot paper to help you.

1

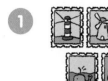  

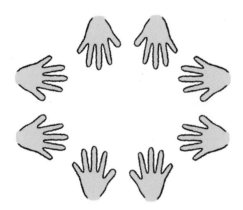

Find 5 groups of 5.

$5 \times 5 =$ _____

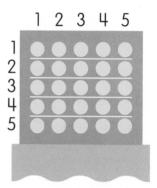

2

Find 8 groups of 5.

$8 \times 5 =$ _____

3

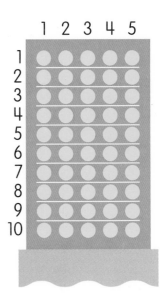

Find 10 groups of 5.

$10 \times 5 =$ _____

Skip count by 5s.
Then, fill in each blank.

4

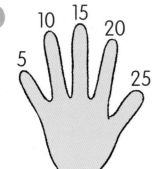

5   10   15   20   25

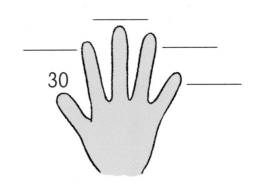

30   _____   _____   _____

Fill in each blank.

5 $3 \times 5 =$ _____

6 $2 \times 5 =$ _____

7 $6 \times 5 =$ _____

8 $8 \times 5 =$ _____

9 $4 \times 5 =$ _____

10 $9 \times 5 =$ _____

11 $1 \times 5 =$ _____

12 $7 \times 5 =$ _____

13 $5 \times 5 =$ _____

14 $10 \times 5 =$ _____

Draw lines to match each wooden plank to its answer.

 15

Color each shape.
Use the same color for the shapes that have the same value.

16

5 × 1

35

1 × 5

20

5 × 7

40

8 × 5

5 × 4

5 × 8

7 × 5

4 × 5

5

3 Multiplying by 10

Learning Objective:
• Skip count by 10s.

THINK

Jane has 120 sticks.
She wants to remove 60 sticks.
How many different ways can she count 60 sticks?

ENGAGE

Draw 3 groups of 10 stars.
What happens after another group of 10 stars is added?
What are two ways you can find the answer?
Explain your thinking to your partner.

Hands-on Activity Skip counting by 10s using a hundreds chart

(1) Circle the number 10.

(2) Start from 10.
Skip count by 10 and circle the numbers.

1	2	3	4	5	6	7	8	9	10
11	12	13	14	15	16	17	18	19	20
21	22	23	24	25	26	27	28	29	30
31	32	33	34	35	36	37	38	39	40
41	42	43	44	45	46	47	48	49	50
51	52	53	54	55	56	57	58	59	60
61	62	63	64	65	66	67	68	69	70
71	72	73	74	75	76	77	78	79	80
81	82	83	84	85	86	87	88	89	90
91	92	93	94	95	96	97	98	99	100

(3) What pattern do you notice?

_____

LEARN Skip count by 10s

1

$1 \times 10 = 10$

$10 + 10 = 20$
$2 \times 10 = 20$

$20 + 10 = 30$
$3 \times 10 = 30$

$30 + 10 = 40$
$4 \times 10 = 40$

$40 + 10 = 50$
$5 \times 10 = 50$

$50 + 10 = 60$
$6 \times 10 = 60$

$60 + 10 = 70$
$7 \times 10 = 70$

$70 + 10 = 80$
$8 \times 10 = 80$

$80 + 10 = 90$
$9 \times 10 = 90$

$90 + 10 = 100$
$10 \times 10 = 100$

I can skip count by adding 10 to get to the next number.

10, 20, 30, 40, 50, 60, 70, 80, 90, 100

I count by 10s.

2 There are 4 bookshelves.
Each bookshelf has 10 books.

4 groups of 10 books
$4 \times 10 = 40$

There are 40 books in all.

1 2 3 4 5 6 7 8 9 10

3 Jane has 7 groups of hairclips.
There are 10 hairclips in each group.

7 groups of 10 hairclips
$7 \times 10 = 70$

There are 70 hairclips in all.

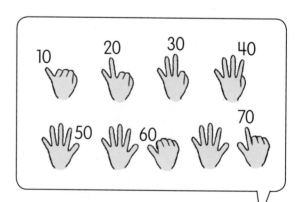

10 20 30 40

50 60 70

 **Math Talk**

Tell your classmates how you find 6×10.
Then, ask your classmate to tell you how he or she finds 9×10.

Multiplication Table of 10

1	×	10	=	10
2	×	10	=	20
3	×	10	=	30
4	×	10	=	40
5	×	10	=	50
6	×	10	=	60
7	×	10	=	70
8	×	10	=	80
9	×	10	=	90
10	×	10	=	100

TRY Practice skip counting by 10s

Fill in each blank.

Find 2 groups of 10.

$2 \times 10 =$ _____

I can skip count by adding 10.

$+ 10$

10 → 20

2

Find 5 groups of 10.

$5 \times 10 =$ _____

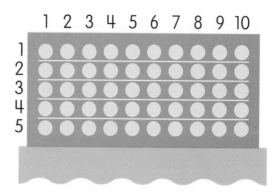

3

Find 8 groups of 10.

$8 \times 10 =$ _____

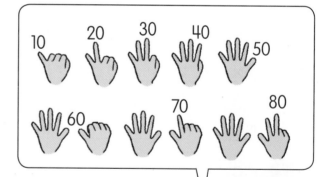
10 20 30 40 50 60 70 80

MULTIPLY AND FILL IN!

What you need:

Players: 2–4

Materials: Multiplication by 2, 5, and 10 cards,
Multiplication worksheets

What to do:

Place the stack of multiplication cards face down.

1. Each player uses a worksheet.

X	1	2	3	4	5	6	7	8	9	10
2										
5										
10										

2. Player 1 draws a card from the multiplication stack.

3. Player 1 writes the answer on the worksheet.

4. The other players check the answer. Players take turns.

Who is the winner?

The first player to fill 20 boxes on the worksheet correctly wins.

Name: _____ Date: _____

INDEPENDENT PRACTICE

Fill in each blank.
Use dot paper to help you.

1

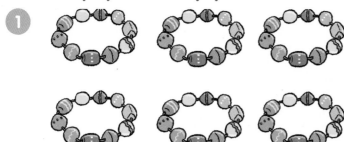

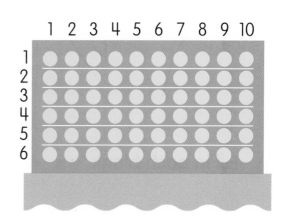

Find 6 groups of 10 beads.

$6 \times 10 =$ _____

2

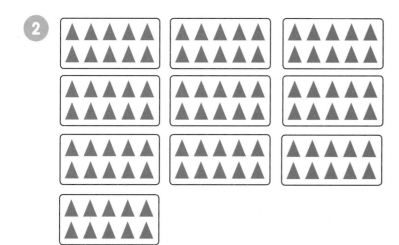

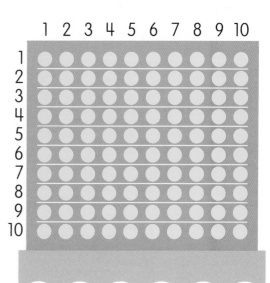

Find 10 groups of 10 triangles.

$10 \times 10 =$ _____

Skip count by 10s.
Then, fill in each blank.

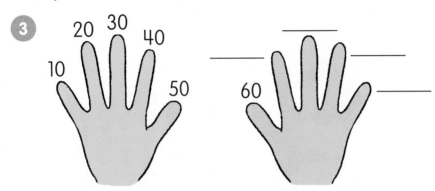

3 20 30 40
10 50 60

Fill in each blank.

4 1 × 1 = _____

1 × 10 = _____

5 6 × 1 = _____

6 × 10 = _____

6 2 × 1 = _____

2 × 10 = _____

7 7 × 1 = _____

7 × 10 = _____

8 3 × 1 = _____

3 × 10 = _____

9 8 × 1 = _____

8 × 10 = _____

10 4 × 1 = _____

4 × 10 = _____

11 9 × 1 = _____

9 × 10 = _____

12 5 × 1 = _____

5 × 10 = _____

13 10 × 1 = _____

10 × 10 = _____

Multiplying by 3

Learning Objectives:
• Skip count by 3s.
• Use known multiplication facts to find other multiplication facts.

THINK

Jane has 24 bookmarks.
She wants to give 15 bookmarks to her brother.
Explain and show different ways she can give her brother 15 bookmarks.

ENGAGE

Kayla has 2 packets of 3 pens.
She buys 1 more packet of 3 pens.
How many pens does she have now?
Use to show your answer in two ways.

LEARN Skip count by 3s

1.

 $1 \times 3 = 3$

 $3 + 3 = 6$
$2 \times 3 = 6$

    $6 + 3 = 9$
$3 \times 3 = 9$

    $9 + 3 = 12$
$4 \times 3 = 12$

 $12 + 3 = 15$
$5 \times 3 = 15$

     $15 + 3 = 18$
$6 \times 3 = 18$

 $18 + 3 = 21$
$7 \times 3 = 21$

 $21 + 3 = 24$
$8 \times 3 = 24$

 $24 + 3 = 27$
$9 \times 3 = 27$

 $27 + 3 = 30$
$10 \times 3 = 30$

Count by 3s: 3, 6, 9, 12, 15, 18, 21, 24, 27, 30.

2 Here are 4 baskets.
3 potatoes are in each basket.

4 groups of 3 potatoes
$4 \times 3 = 12$

There are 12 potatoes in all.

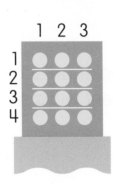

3 There are 6 groups.
Each group has 3 buttons.

6 groups of 3 buttons
$6 \times 3 = 18$

There are 18 buttons in all.

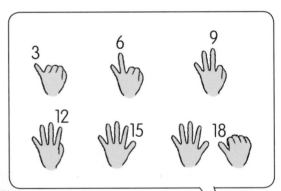

Math Talk

Tell your partner how you find 8×3.
Then, ask your partner to tell you
how he or she finds 9×3.

TRY Practice skip counting by 3s

Fill in each blank.

1

I can skip count by adding 3.

$$3 \xrightarrow{+3} 6$$

Find 2 groups of 3.

$2 \times 3 =$ _____

2

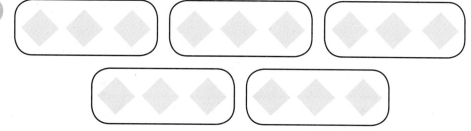

Find 5 groups of 3.

$5 \times 3 =$ _____

3

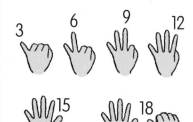

3   6   9   12

15   18

21   24

Find 8 groups of 3.

$8 \times 3 =$ _____

ENGAGE

There are 5 plates of 3 strawberries on the table.
How many strawberries are there in all?
Malia puts another plate of 3 strawberries on the table.
How many strawberries are there now?
Explain to your partner the steps you took to find your answer.

LEARN Use known multiplication facts to find other multiplication facts

1. $6 \times 3 = ?$

Start with 5 groups of 3.

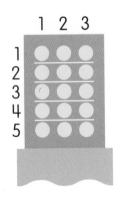 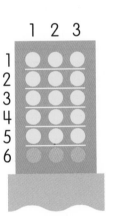

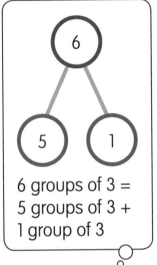

6 groups of 3 =
5 groups of 3 +
1 group of 3

$$5 \times 3 = 15$$

$$6 \times 3 = 15 + 3$$
$$= 18$$

Math Talk

Can you find 7×3 from 5×3?
Show your partner how you do it.
Use the dot paper to help you.

2 $8 \times 3 = ?$

Start with 10 groups of 3.

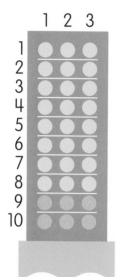

$10 \times 3 = 30$

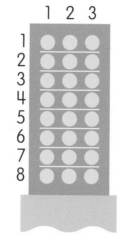

$8 \times 3 = 30 - 6$
$\qquad = 24$

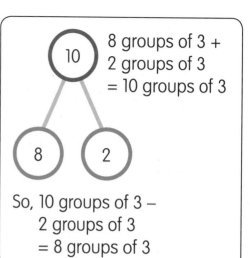

8 groups of 3 +
2 groups of 3
= 10 groups of 3

So, 10 groups of 3 −
2 groups of 3
= 8 groups of 3

Multiplication Table of 3

1	×	3	=	3
2	×	3	=	6
3	×	3	=	9
4	×	3	=	12
5	×	3	=	15
6	×	3	=	18
7	×	3	=	21
8	×	3	=	24
9	×	3	=	27
10	×	3	=	30

Math Talk

Can you find 9×3 from 10×3?
Show your partner how you do it.
Use the dot paper to help you.

TRY Practice using known multiplication facts to find other multiplication facts

Fill in each blank.
Use dot paper to help you.

1 $7 \times 3 = ?$

 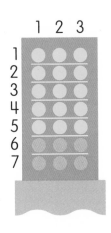

$5 \times 3 = $ _____

$7 \times 3 = 15 + $ _____

$= $ _____

2 $9 \times 3 = ?$

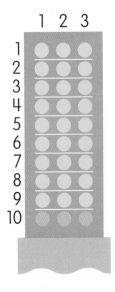 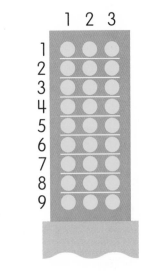

$10 \times 3 = $ _____

$9 \times 3 = 30 - $ _____

$= $ _____

INDEPENDENT PRACTICE

Fill in each blank.
Use dot paper to help you.

Find 3 groups of 3.

_____ × _____ = _____

 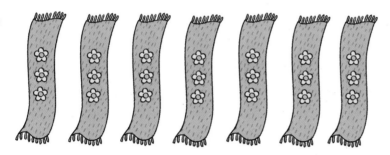

Find 7 groups of 3.

$7 \times 3 =$ _____

 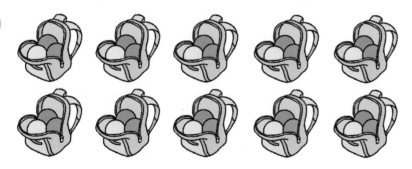 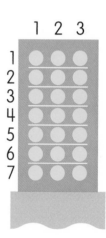

Find 10 groups of 3.

$10 \times 3 =$ _____

Skip count by 3s.
Then, fill in each blank.

4
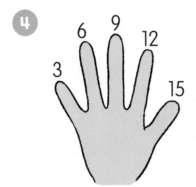
3 6 9 12 15

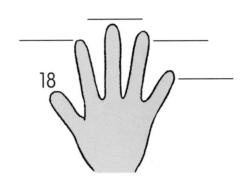
18

Fill in each blank.

5 4 × 3 = _____

6 2 × 3 = _____

7 6 × 3 = _____

8 8 × 3 = _____

9 5 × 3 = _____

10 9 × 3 = _____

11 7 × 3 = _____

12 1 × 3 = _____

13 3 × 3 = _____

14 10 × 3 = _____

Fill in each blank.
Use dot paper to help you.

15 4 × 3 = _____

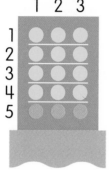

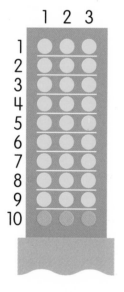

_____ × _____ = _____

4 × 3 = _____ – _____

= _____

16 9 × 3 = _____

_____ × _____ = _____

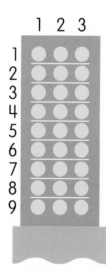

9 × 3 = _____ – _____

= _____

Draw lines to match each wooden plank to its shape.

 17

 6 × 3 •

 24 •

 4 × 3 •

18 •

 5 × 3 •

30 •

 10 × 3 •

12 •

 8 × 3 •

15 •

5 Multiplying by 4

Learning Objectives:
• Skip count by 4s.
• Use known multiplication facts to find other multiplication facts.

THINK

Mr. Jones buys 36 eggs.
He wants to use 16 eggs for cooking.
Explain and show different ways he can count 16 eggs.

What information do I know?
What do I need to find out?
What method can I use?

ENGAGE

a   What is 4 + 4?

b   Find 4 + 4 + 4 in two different ways.
What is another way to find:

i   5 groups of 4?

ii   6 groups of 4?

Explain your thinking to your partner.

1 Use ● to show two sets of 1 × 2.
Add to find the total number of ● in the two sets.

2 Fill in the table.
Repeat 1 for the rest of the multiplication table of 2.

	Number of ● in each set	Total number of ● in the two sets
1 × 2		
2 × 2		
3 × 2		
4 × 2		
5 × 2		
6 × 2		
7 × 2		
8 × 2		
9 × 2		
10 × 2		

2 + 2 = 4
The double of 2 is 4.
When you double the multiplication table of 2,
the answer is the multiplication table of 4!

LEARN Skip count by 4s

$$1 \times 4 = 4$$

$$20 + 4 = 24$$
$$6 \times 4 = 24$$

$$4 + 4 = 8$$
$$2 \times 4 = 8$$

$$24 + 4 = 28$$
$$7 \times 4 = 28$$

$$8 + 4 = 12$$
$$3 \times 4 = 12$$

$$28 + 4 = 32$$
$$8 \times 4 = 32$$

$$12 + 4 = 16$$
$$4 \times 4 = 16$$

$$32 + 4 = 36$$
$$9 \times 4 = 36$$

$$16 + 4 = 20$$
$$5 \times 4 = 20$$

$$36 + 4 = 40$$
$$10 \times 4 = 40$$

I can skip count by adding 4 to get to the next number.

4, 8, 12, 16, 20, 24, 28, 32, 36, 40

I count by 4s.

2 There are 5 stacks of books.
Each stack has 4 books.

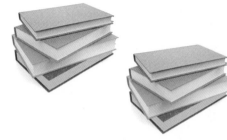

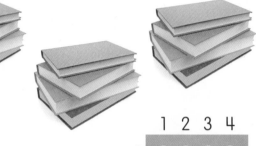

5 groups of 4 books
$5 \times 4 = 20$

There are 20 books in all.

3 Mr. Lee has 7 groups of yarn.
There are 4 balls of yarn in each group.

7 groups of 4 balls of yarn
$7 \times 4 = 28$

There are 28 balls of yarn in all.

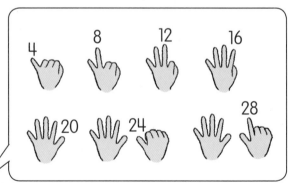

TRY Practice skip counting by 4

Fill in each blank.

1

Find 3 groups of 4.

3 × 4 = _____

I can skip count by adding 4.

+ 4   + 4

4   8   12

2

Find 6 groups of 4.

6 × 4 = _____

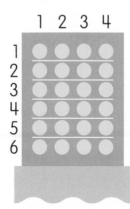

3

Find 9 groups of 4.

$9 \times 4 =$ _____

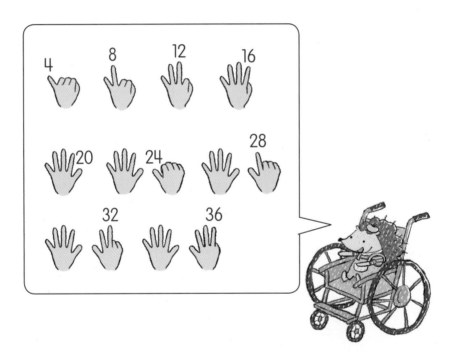

ENGAGE

Ms. Davis has 10 bags of 4 oranges.
She gives one bag of oranges to her neighbor.
How many oranges does Ms. Davis have now?
Explain to your partner the steps you took to find your answer.

LEARN Use known multiplication facts to find other multiplication facts

1 $6 \times 4 = ?$

Start with 5 groups of 4.

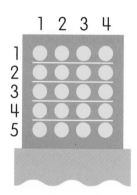

$5 \times 4 = 20$

$6 \times 4 = 20 + 4$
$= 24$

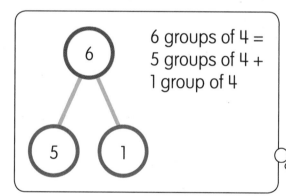

6 groups of 4 =
5 groups of 4 +
1 group of 4

Math Talk
Can you find 7×4 from 5×4?
Show your partner how you do it.
Use the dot paper to help you.

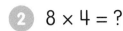
2 $8 \times 4 = ?$

Start with 10 groups of 4.

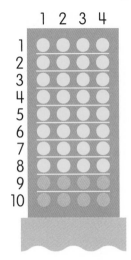

$10 \times 4 = 40$

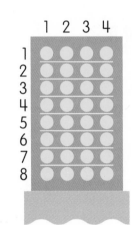

$8 \times 4 = 40 - 8$
$= 32$

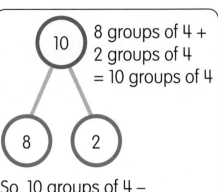

8 groups of 4 +
2 groups of 4
= 10 groups of 4

So, 10 groups of 4 −
2 groups of 4
= 8 groups of 4

Multiplication Table of 4

1	×	4	=	4
2	×	4	=	8
3	×	4	=	12
4	×	4	=	16
5	×	4	=	20
6	×	4	=	24
7	×	4	=	28
8	×	4	=	32
9	×	4	=	36
10	×	4	=	40

Math Talk

Can you find 7×4 from 10×4?
Show your partner how you do it.
Use the dot paper to help you.

TRY Practice using known multiplication facts to find other multiplication facts

Fill in each blank.
Use dot paper to help you.

1 $7 \times 4 = ?$

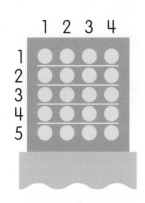 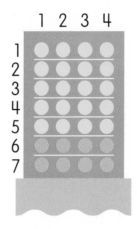

$5 \times 4 =$ _____

$7 \times 4 = 20 +$ _____

$=$ _____

2 $9 \times 4 = ?$

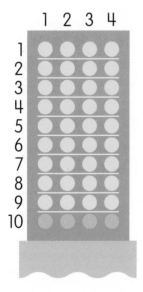 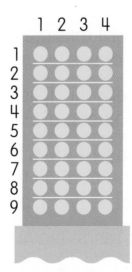

$10 \times 4 =$ _____

$9 \times 4 = 40 -$ _____

$=$ _____

NUMBER SUBMARINE!

What you need:

Players: 4–6
Materials: Number submarine, Number cards (2, 3, and 4), one 🎲

What to do:

Place the number cards face down.

1 Player 1 rolls the number cube and draws a number card.

> 32, 9, 4, 16, 18, 36, 24, 21, 10 28, 12, 14, 8, 18, 6, 20, 10, 4

2 Player 1 multiplies the two numbers. The other players check the answer.

3 If Player 1 gives the correct answer, he or she circles the number on the number submarine. If not, Player 1 loses his or her turn.

4 Rearrange the number cards.

5 Take turns to play. Repeat **1** to **4**.

Who is the winner?

The first player to circle all the numbers on the number submarine wins.

INDEPENDENT PRACTICE

Fill in each blank.
Use dot paper to help you.

1

Find 4 groups of 4.

4 × 4 = _____

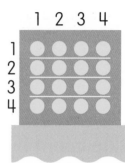

2

Find 8 groups of 4.

8 × 4 = _____

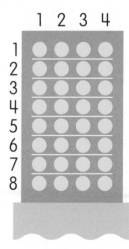

 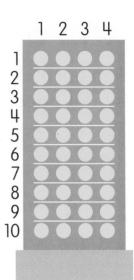

Find 10 groups of 4.

_____ × _____ = _____

Skip count by 4s.
Then, fill in each blank.

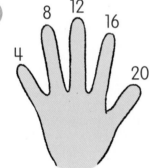

Fill in each blank.

5 3 × 4 = _____

6 6 × 4 = _____

7 2 × 4 = _____

8 8 × 4 = _____

9 1 × 4 = _____

10 9 × 4 = _____

11 5 × 4 = _____

12 4 × 4 = _____

13 10 × 4 = _____

14 7 × 4 = _____

Fill in each blank.
Use dot paper to help you.

15 3 × 4 = _____

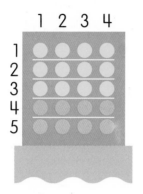

_____ × _____ = _____

3 × 4 = _____ − _____

= _____

16 9 × 4 = _____

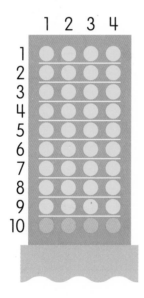

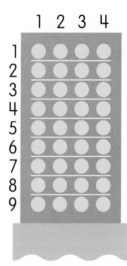

_____ × _____ = _____

9 × 4 = _____ − _____

= _____

Draw lines to match each wooden plank to its answer.

17

 8 × 4 •

•  4 groups of 4

 7 × 4 •

•  2 groups of 4

 2 × 4 •

•  7 groups of 4

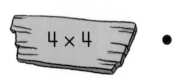 4 × 4 •

•  8 groups of 4

Name: _____ Date: _____

6 Multiplying Numbers in Any Order

Learning Objective:
• Understand that multiplication can be done in any order.

New Vocabulary
related
multiplication facts

THINK

List all the multiplication facts that give 12.
Give an example of multiplication fact family.

ENGAGE

a Count 5 groups of 3 pencils.
Ask your partner to count 3 groups of 5 pencils.
Compare the number of pencils each of you have.
What do you notice?

b Joseph has 3 groups of 7 eggs.
What is another way to show the eggs?

LEARN Multiply numbers in any order

1 These are related multiplication facts.

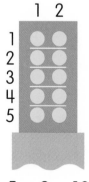

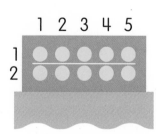

$5 \times 2 = 10$ $2 \times 5 = 10$

$2 \times 5 = 5 \times 2$

2

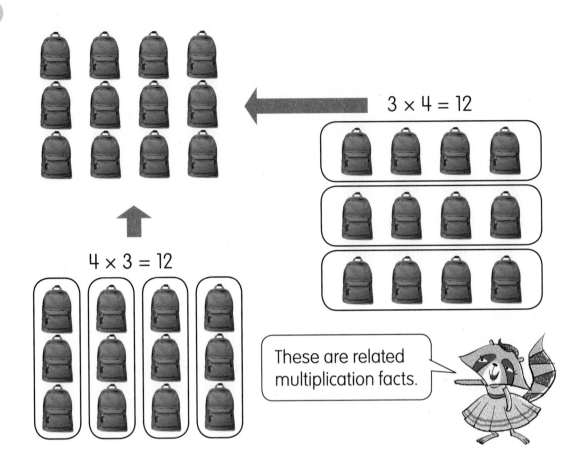

$3 \times 4 = 12$

$4 \times 3 = 12$

These are related multiplication facts.

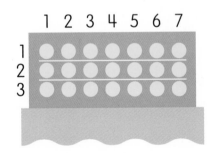

TRY Practice multiplying numbers in any order

Fill in each blank.

1

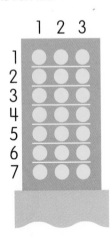

_____ × _____ = 21

_____ × _____ = 21

2

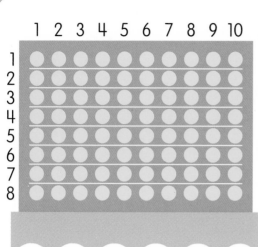

_____ × _____ = 80

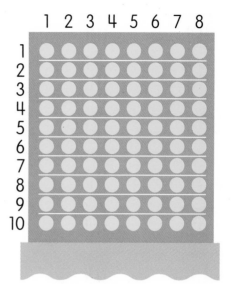

_____ × _____ = 80

3

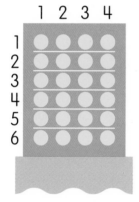

_____ × _____ = 24

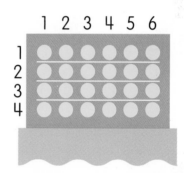

_____ × _____ = 24

4

_____ × _____ = 20

_____ × _____ = 20

5

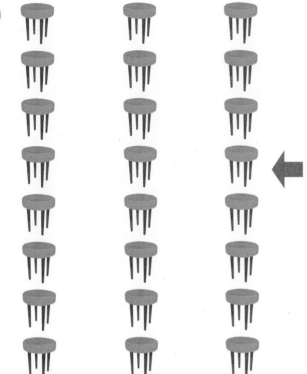

←————— _____ × _____ = 27

↑

_____ × _____ = 27

6

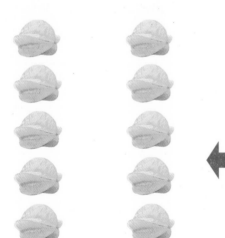

←————— _____ × _____ = 12

↑

_____ × _____ = 12

INDEPENDENT PRACTICE

Fill in each blank.

1

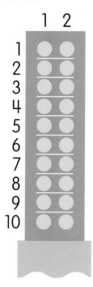

_____ × _____ = _____   _____ × _____ = _____

2

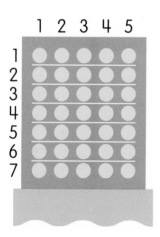

_____ × _____ = _____   _____ × _____ = _____

3

   ← _____ × _____ = _____

↑

_____ × _____ = _____

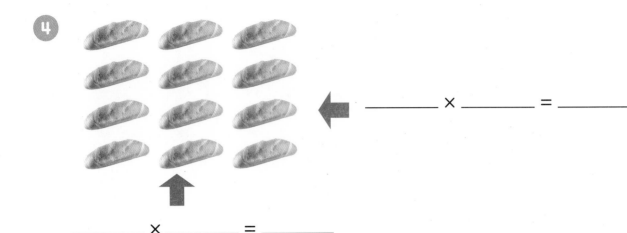

4

$$\underline{\hspace{2cm}} \times \underline{\hspace{2cm}} = \underline{\hspace{2cm}}$$

$$\underline{\hspace{2cm}} \times \underline{\hspace{2cm}} = \underline{\hspace{2cm}}$$

Match each wooden plank to its answer.

5

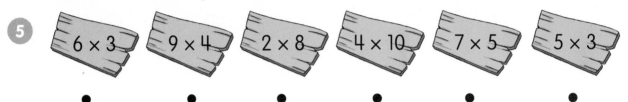

6 × 3   9 × 4   2 × 8   4 × 10   7 × 5   5 × 3

36   18   40   16   15   35

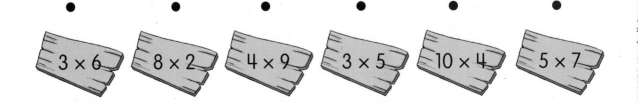

3 × 6   8 × 2   4 × 9   3 × 5   10 × 4   5 × 7

7 Dividing Using Multiplication Facts

Learning Objectives:
• Use multiplication facts to find related division facts.
• Write fact families of multiplication and division.

> **New Vocabulary**
> related multiplication and division facts

THINK

Billy has 27 picture cards.
He wants to share the cards equally among his friends.
What is the greatest possible number of cards each friend will receive?

ENGAGE

Rearrange the ⬤ and ◯ into equal groups.
Show all the ways you can do this.
Draw a picture to show your thinking.

LEARN Divide using multiplication facts

1 Divide 28 plates equally into 4 groups.

$28 \div 4 = ?$

> $7 \times 4 = 28$
> So, $28 \div 4 = 7$.

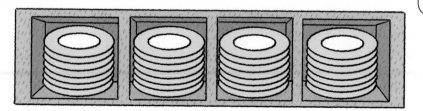

There are 7 plates in each group.

© 2020 Marshall Cavendish Education Pte Ltd

2 Divide 15 apples equally into groups of 5.

15 ÷ 5 = ?

$3 \times 5 = 15$
So, $15 \div 5 = 3$

There are 3 groups.

TRY Practice dividing using multiplication facts

Fill in each blank.

1 Divide 8 strawberry tarts equally among 4 people.

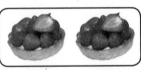
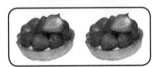

_____ × 4 = 8

So, $8 \div 4 =$ _____.

$8 \div 4 =$ _____

Each person gets _____ strawberry tarts.

2 Divide 21 glasses of juice equally into trays of 3.

_____ × 3 = 21

So, $21 \div 3 =$ _____.

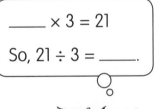

$21 \div 3 =$ _____

There are _____ trays.

3 Put 16 ribbons equally into 2 groups.

16 ÷ 2 = _____

There are _____ ribbons in each group.

_____ × 2 = 16

So, 16 ÷ 2 = _____.

4 Divide 20 beads into equal groups.
There are 10 beads in each group.

20 ÷ 10 = _____

There are _____ groups of beads.

_____ × 10 = 20

So, 20 ÷ 10 = _____.

ENGAGE

a Take 18 .
Arrange them into equal groups.
Then, write a multiplication fact and a division fact.

b Next, group the in another way.
Then, write a different multiplication fact and a division fact.

LEARN Make multiplication and division fact families

1 Some toy bears are arranged on shelves.

a How many toy bears are there?

$3 \times 2 = 6$ or $2 \times 3 = 6$
There are 6 toy bears.

b How many shelves are there?

$6 \div 2 = 3$
There are 3 shelves.

c How many toy bears are there on each shelf?

$6 \div 3 = 2$
There are 2 toy bears on each shelf.

2 These are related multiplication and division facts.

$3 \times 2 = 6$ $2 \times 3 = 6$ $6 \div 2 = 3$ $6 \div 3 = 2$

Hands-on Activity Making multiplication and division fact families

Work in pairs.

① Write a multiplication sentence.

_____ × _____ = _____

② Ask your partner to write the other family facts.

_____ × _____ = _____

_____ ÷ _____ = _____

_____ ÷ _____ = _____

③ Trade places. Repeat ① to ②.

_____ × _____ = _____

_____ × _____ = _____

_____ ÷ _____ = _____

_____ ÷ _____ = _____

TRY Practice making multiplication and division fact families

Make a fact family for each picture.

①

_____ × _____ = _____   _____ ÷ _____ = _____

_____ × _____ = _____   _____ ÷ _____ = _____

2

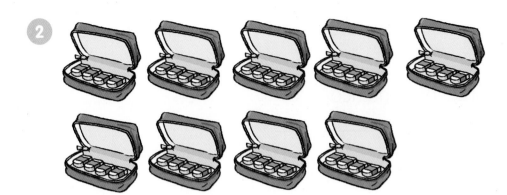

_____ × _____ = _____   _____ ÷ _____ = _____

_____ × _____ = _____   _____ ÷ _____ = _____

3

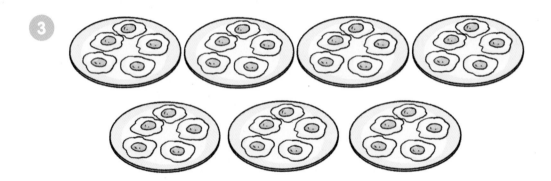

_____ × _____ = _____   _____ ÷ _____ = _____

_____ × _____ = _____   _____ ÷ _____ = _____

4

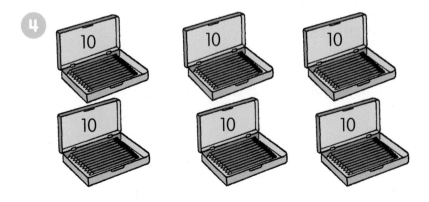

_____ × _____ = _____   _____ ÷ _____ = _____

_____ × _____ = _____   _____ ÷ _____ = _____

INDEPENDENT PRACTICE

Fill in each blank.

1. Put 12 badges equally into packets of 2.

   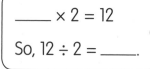

_____ × 2 = 12

So, 12 ÷ 2 = _____.

_____ ÷ _____ = _____

There are _____ packets.

2. Share 35 strawberries equally among 5 children.

_____ ÷ _____ = _____

Each child receives _____ strawberries.

3. Place 24 spoons equally into 3 rows.

_____ ÷ _____ = _____

There are _____ spoons in each row.

Make a family fact for each picture.

_____ × _____ = _____

_____ × _____ = _____

_____ ÷ 3 = _____

_____ ÷ _____ = _____

5

_____ × _____ = _____

_____ × _____ = _____

_____ ÷ _____ = _____

_____ ÷ _____ = _____

6 **Write a fact family for these numbers.**

_____ × _____ = _____

_____ × _____ = _____

_____ ÷ _____ = _____

_____ ÷ _____ = _____

Name: _____   Date: _____

Mathematical Habit 3 **Construct viable arguments**

Mr. Diaz has 12 buttons.
He wants to put them equally into small groups.

Show two different ways that he can put the buttons into small groups.
Draw pictures to help you.

Problem Solving with Heuristics

1 **Mathematical Habit 8** Look for patterns

Sara has a multiplying machine.
It multiplies the number she puts in by a number.
The new number comes out of the machine.
She puts in six numbers from 1 to 10.
Four numbers come out of the machine.
Two numbers are still inside the machine.

a By what number does the machine multiply the numbers put in?

b Sara wants to use the six numbers to make a number pattern. What are the two numbers that are still in the machine?

c Write the number pattern that Sara makes.

2 **Mathematical Habit 1** Persevere in solving problems

I am a 2-digit number.
I am greater than 10.
I am also smaller than 17.
I can be found in the multiplication table of 2.
What numbers can I be?

First, write the multiplication table of 2.

3 **Mathematical Habit** **1** **Persevere in solving problems**

Ethan has fewer than 12 crayons.
He puts all of them into bundles.
He puts 2 crayons in each bundle.
No crayons are left.
How many crayons does Ethan have?

There is more than one answer.

CHAPTER WRAP-UP

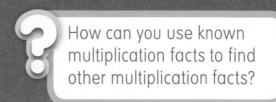

? How can you use known multiplication facts to find other multiplication facts?

Multiplication Tables

Multiplying by 2

a skip counting by 2s

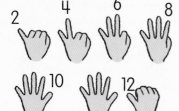

b using known multiplication facts

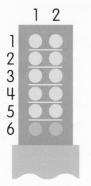

$6 \times 2 = 10 + 2$
$= 12$

Multiplying by 5

skip counting by 5s

$7 \times 5 = 35$

Multiplying by 10

skip counting by 10s

$3 \times 10 = 30$

| Multiplying by 3 | Multiplying by 4 | Multiplying Numbers in Any Order | Dividing |

a skip counting by 3s

3   6   9

12   15

18   21

24

a skip counting by 4s

4   8   12

16   20   24

28   32

36

You can multiply numbers in any order.

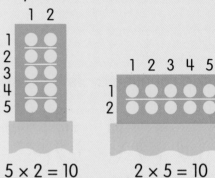

$5 \times 2 = 10$ $2 \times 5 = 10$

a You can use multiplication facts to divide.
$3 \times 4 = 12$
So, $12 \div 4 = 3$

b This is a fact family of multiplication and division.
$3 \times 4 = 12$
$4 \times 3 = 12$
$12 \div 4 = 3$
$12 \div 3 = 4$

b using known multiplication facts

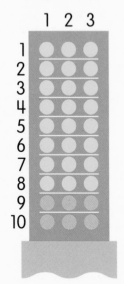

$8 \times 3 = 30 - 6$
$\quad\quad = 24$

b using known multiplication facts

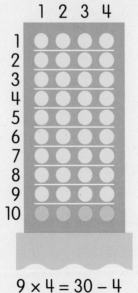

$9 \times 4 = 30 - 4$
$\quad\quad = 36$

Name: _____ Date: _____

Answer each question.

1. 6 groups of 2 = _____

2. 9 groups of 5 = _____

3. 7 × 4 = _____

4. 3 × 9 = _____

5. 24 ÷ 3 = _____

6. 5 × 10 = _____

Color all the statements that describe the picture.

7.

| 8 groups of 5 | 5 groups of 8 | 40 ÷ 5 = 8 |

Answer each question.

8. 2 × 3 = _____
   3 × 2 = _____

9. 6 × 4 = _____
   4 × 6 = _____

10. 7 × 5 = _____
    5 × 7 = _____

11. 3 × 10 = _____
    10 × 3 = _____

12. 9 × 2 = _____
    2 × 9 = _____

13. 6 × 5 = _____
    5 × 6 = _____

Answer each question.

14) _____ × 2 = 18

15) _____ × 2 = 10

16) _____ × 3 = 12

17) _____ × 3 = 18

18) _____ × 4 = 32

19) _____ × 4 = 28

20) _____ × 5 = 15

21) _____ × 5 = 45

22) _____ × 10 = 20

23) _____ × 10 = 100

Fill in each blank.
Then, write a different division sentence.

24) _____ × 2 = 14

14 ÷ 2 = _____

14 ÷ _____ = _____

25) _____ × 3 = 27

27 ÷ 3 = _____

27 ÷ _____ = _____

26) _____ × 4 = 12

12 ÷ 4 = _____

12 ÷ _____ = _____

27) _____ × 5 = 40

40 ÷ 5 = _____

40 ÷ _____ = _____

28) _____ × 10 = 60

60 ÷ 10 = _____

60 ÷ _____ = _____

Fill in each blank.

29 Find 4 groups of 4.

_____ × _____ = _____

There are _____ squirrels in all.

30 Divide 24 flowers equally into 4 vases.

_____ ÷ _____ = _____

There are _____ flowers in each vase.

31 Divide 70 stamps into equal groups.
There are 10 stamps in each group.

$70 ÷ 10 =$ _____

There are _____ groups of stamps.

32 Look at the picture.
Which of these correctly describes the picture?

(A) 3 × 2 = 6

(B) 4 × 2 = 8

(C) 5 × 2 = 10

(D) 7 × 2 = 14

33 Evan puts 20 sticks equally into 5 bundles.
How many sticks are there in each bundle?

(A) 20

(B) 15

(C) 5

(D) 4

Name: _____ Date: _____

Counting Toys

1 Diego made 3 paper boats each day for his art class. How many paper boats did he make in 5 days?

Color the boxes that show the number of paper boats Diego made in 5 days.

$3 + 3 + 3 + 3 + 3$ or $5 + 5 + 5$

3 groups of 5   or   5 groups of 3

5×3 or 5×15

He made _____ paper boats in 5 days.

2 Find the value of .

 × 5 = 50   = _____

Complete the addition sentences below.

 = _____

_____ + _____ + _____ + _____ + _____ + _____

= _____

Complete the multiplication sentences below.

6 × = _____

_____ × _____ = _____

3 A group of 4 children went to a toy fair.
Each child bought 2 toys.
How many toys did the children buy in all?
Fill in the missing numbers.

_____ + _____ + _____ + _____ = _____

_____ × _____ = _____

The children bought _____ toys in all.

4 Ms. Green has 9 boxes of wooden blocks.
There are 4 wooden blocks in each box.
How many wooden blocks does Ms. Green have in all?
Write a multiplication sentence.

Ms. Green has _____ wooden blocks in all.
How did you get your answer?

Rubric

Point(s)	Level	My Performance
7–8	4	• Most of my answers are correct. • I show all my work correctly. • I explain my thinking clearly and completely.
5–6.5	3	• Some of my answers are correct. • I show some of my work correctly. • I explain my thinking clearly.
3–4.5	2	• A few of my answers are correct. • I show little work correctly. • I explain some of my thinking clearly.
0–2.5	1	• A few of my answers are correct. • I show little or no work. • I do not explain my thinking clearly.

Teacher's Comments

Chapter 10

Time and Money

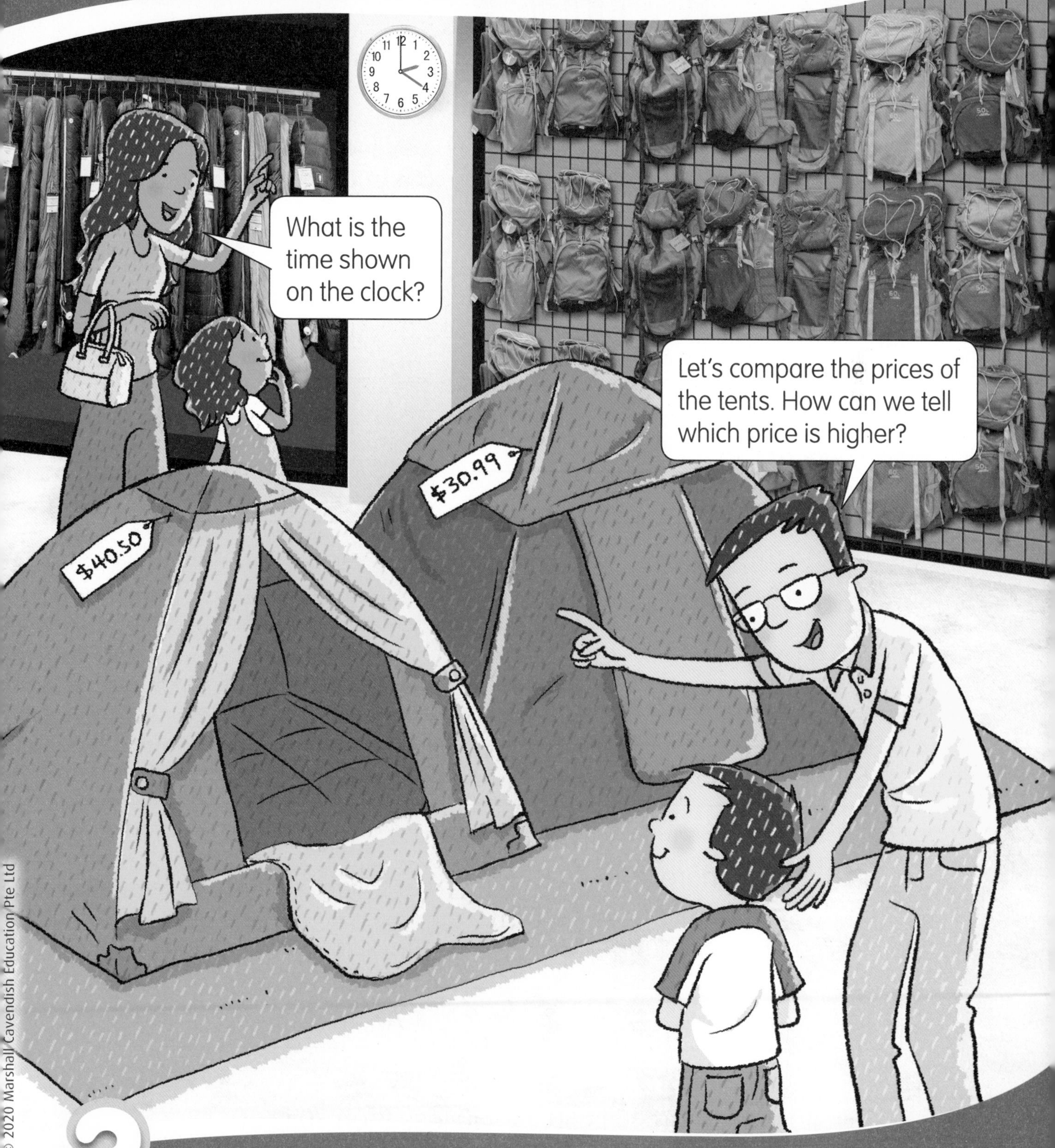

11 12 1 10 2 9 3 8 4 7 6 5
What is the time shown on the clock?
Let's compare the prices of the tents. How can we tell which price is higher?
$30.99
$40.50

How can you tell time in different ways?
When do you use addition and subtraction in money?

Name: _____   Date: _____

Skip counting by 5s and 10s

a

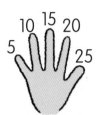   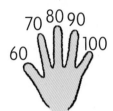

b

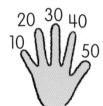

▶ **Quick Check**

Fill in each blank.

1 15, 20, 25, 30, _____, _____, _____

2 40, 50, 60, _____, _____, _____

Finding numbers in a pattern by adding or subtracting

a

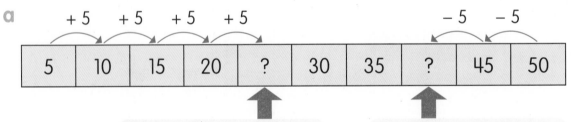

5 more than 20 is 25.   5 less than 45 is 40.

b

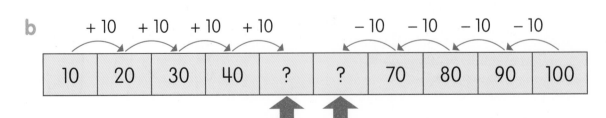

10 more than 40 is 50.   10 less than 70 is 60.

▶ **Quick Check**

Find each missing number.

③ 10 is 5 more than _____ .

④ 25 is 10 less than _____ .

Telling time

a

It is 9 o'clock.

b

7:30

It is half past 7.

▶ **Quick Check**

Write each time.

⑤

_____

⑥

_____

⑦ 11:00

_____

⑧ 9:30

_____

Types of coins

  or   These are the two faces of a penny.
A penny has a value of 1 cent.

  or   These are the two faces of a nickel.
A nickel has a value of 5 cents.

  These are the two faces of a dime.
A dime has a value of 10 cents.

  These are the two faces of a quarter.
A quarter has a value of 25 cents.

These are also quarters.

▶ **Quick Check**

Write the value of each coin.

(9) _____ ¢

(10) _____ ¢

(11) _____ ¢

(12) _____ ¢

Exchanging coins

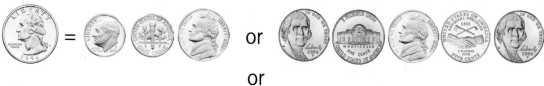

or

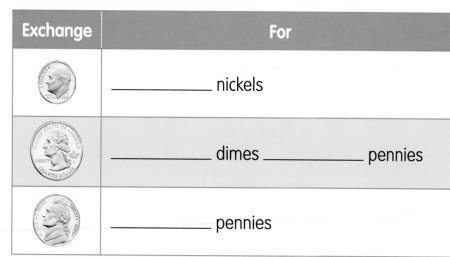

▶ Quick Check

Fill in each blank.

(13)	Exchange	For
		_____ nickels
		_____ dimes _____ pennies
		_____ pennies

Combining coins to show a given amount

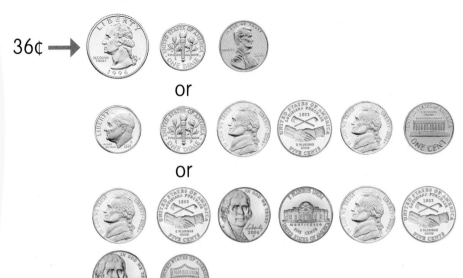

36¢ →

or

or

▶ Quick Check

Fill in each blank.

14   _____ ¢

15   _____ ¢

Circle the coins to make the given value.

16 85¢

17 55¢

Reading and Writing Time

Learning Objectives:
- Use the minute hand to show and tell time for every five minutes after the hour.
- Show and tell time in hours and minutes.

> **New Vocabulary**
> minute   clock face
> hour   after

THINK

Mr. Stewart leaves his house at 1 o'clock.
He drives and arrives at the zoo at 2 o'clock if he does not stop along the way.
How can you tell the time if he stops along the way to get a drink?
What is another way to tell the time?

ENGAGE

a   Caleb counts by 10 using the clock shown below.

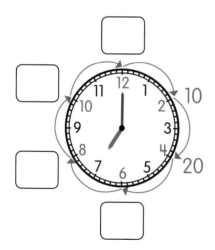

b   Use  to show 15 minutes after the time shown above.

LEARN Skip count by 5s to tell the time

1 You can skip count by 5s to find how many minutes have passed.

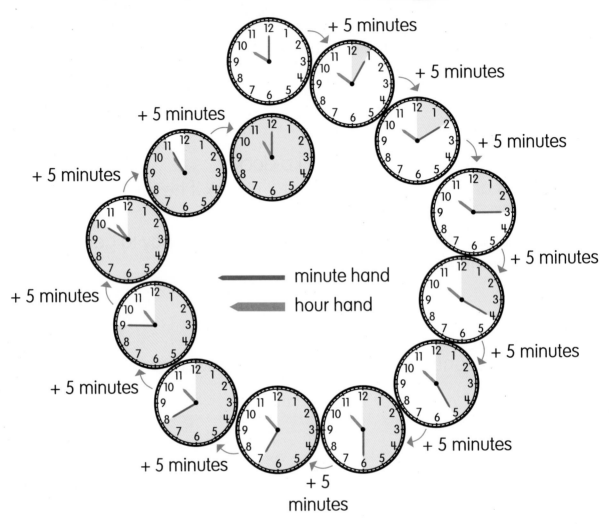

minute hand

hour hand

+ 5 minutes

There are 60 minutes in 1 hour.

The minute hand takes 60 minutes to move around the
clock face once.
The hour hand takes 1 hour to move from 10 to 11.

2 You can use the numbers on the clock to skip count by 5s starting from 12.

8 o'clock → 5 minutes later → 5 minutes after 8 o'clock

8 o'clock → 40 minutes later → 40 minutes after 8 o'clock

I count by fives. 5, 10, 15, 20, 25, 30, 35, 40.

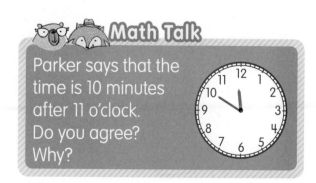

Math Talk

Parker says that the time is 10 minutes after 11 o'clock. Do you agree? Why?

Hands-on Activity ▸ Showing and telling the time

Work in pairs.

(1) Use 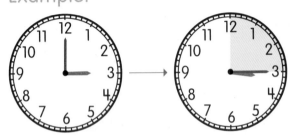 to show time to the hour.

(2) Your partner will say the minutes after the hour.

(3) Skip count by 5s to show the time.

(4) Your partner will say the time using minutes, after and o'clock.

Example:

It is 3 o'clock.　　It is 15 minutes after 3 o'clock.

What do you notice about the minutes when you skip count by 5s?

(5) Tell your partner what you do at that time of the day in (4).

I do my homework at 15 minutes after 3 o'clock.

(6) Trade places. Repeat (1) to (5).

Fill in each blank.
Skip count by 5s to help you.

1

_____ minutes later

8 o'clock   _____ minutes after 8 o'clock

2

_____ minutes after 10 o'clock

3

_____ minutes after 2 o'clock

Draw the minute hand on each clock to show the time.

4

10 minutes after 4 o'clock

5

55 minutes after 8 o'clock

ENGAGE

Use to show 25 minutes after 9 o'clock.

What other ways can you tell the time?

Explain your answer.

LEARN Tell and write time in hours and minutes

1 Anya, Alexis, Sergio and Jaden are going on a field trip.
They cannot wait to get to school!

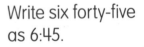

6:35

My school bus will arrive at six thirty-five.

Write six thirty-five as 6:35.

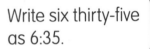

6:45

It is six forty-five. The bus is not here yet!

Write six forty-five as 6:45.

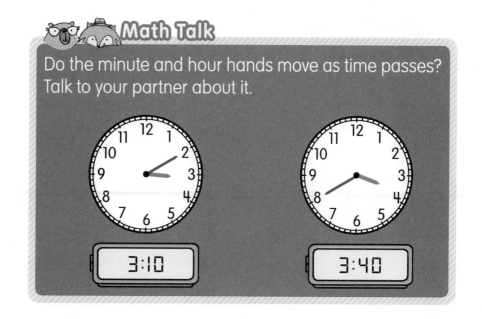

TRY Practice telling and writing time in hours and minutes

Draw the minute hand on each clock to show the time.

1 4:20

2 5:35

Write each time.

3

_____

4

_____

5

_____

6

_____

7

10:40

_____

8

4:15

_____

INDEPENDENT PRACTICE

Look at the minute hand.
Fill in each blank.

_____ minutes

_____ minutes

Fill in each blank.
Skip count by 5s to help you.

_____ minutes after 5 o'clock

_____ minutes after 8 o'clock

Draw the minute hand on each clock to show the time.

15 minutes after 1 o'clock

50 minutes after 11 o'clock

7   8:45

 **8**   1:00

Write each time.

 9

_____

10

_____

11

_____

12

_____

13   6:35

_____

14   5:05

_____

Name: _____ Date: _____

2 Using A.M. and P.M.

Learning Objectives:
- Use A.M. and P.M. to show morning, afternoon, or night.
- Order events by time.

New Vocabulary
A.M.
P.M.

THINK

Felipe did the activities below in a day.

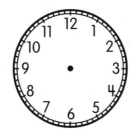

He took a nap at two twenty-five.

He took his breakfast at _____.

He walked his dog at six thirty.

What is a possible time that Felipe had his breakfast?
Do you use A.M. or P.M. to tell each time?

ENGAGE

Kwan has his breakfast at 6:15 in the morning.
He has his dinner at 6:15 in the evening.
Show each time on the clock.
What is the difference?

LEARN Use A.M. and P.M.

1 Nicolas wants to watch a movie. The movie starts at twelve fifteen in the afternoon or 12:15 P.M.

> P.M. is used to talk about time just after noon to just before midnight.

He has to leave the house earlier than that time.

He leaves the house at eleven forty in the morning or 11:40 A.M.

> A.M. is used to talk about time just after midnight to just before noon.

2 Evelyn plans her birthday party by order of time.

Evelyn changes into her new dress at 10:15 A.M.

Evelyn welcomes her friends at 11:00 A.M.

Evelyn and her friends have their lunch at 12:45 P.M.

They play games at 2:25 P.M.

Her friends sing her a birthday song at 3:50 P.M.

Her birthday party ends at 4:30 P.M.

TRY Practice using A.M. and P.M.

Look at the pictures.
Fill in each blank with A.M. or P.M.

1

Ava plays with Zoe until
6:00 _____
Then, Ava returns home.

2

After dinner, Ava does her homework.
Then, she goes to bed
at 8:30 _____

3

Ava wakes up at
7:00 _____
She has breakfast and goes
to school.

4

After school, Ava goes
to Zoe's house at
2:00 _____

Look at the pictures.
Fill in each box with 1, 2, 3, 4, 5, and 6 to put them in the
right order.

5 The Kim family goes to a water park.

They compete against
each other on the body
slide at 3:25 P.M.

Dylan and Claire are
splashing about in the
pool at 5:05 P.M.

They reach the water park to buy tickets at 2:40 P.M.

Mr. Kim drives the family to the water park at 1:35 P.M.

Before heading home, they have some sandwiches at 5:55 P.M.

They scream in joy as they play the raft slide at 4:20 P.M.

Mathematical Habit 6 Use precise mathematical language

Choose a day of the week.

Describe what you did at these times.

1 7:00 A.M.   **2** 10:15 A.M.   **3** 12:30 P.M.   **4** 6:40 P.M.

MATH SHARING

IDENTIFY THEM!

When do most people have their dinner?

What you need:

Players: 2
Materials: A.M. or P.M. Activity cards

What to do:

Place the deck of activity cards face down.

1. Player 1 turns over a card and reads the activity to Player 2.

2. Player 2 uses A.M. or P.M. to tell the time of the day.

3. Player 1 checks the answer.
   Player 2 gets a point if the answer is correct.

4. Trade places. Repeat 1 to 3.

Who is the winner?

The player with more points after 5 rounds wins.

Name: _____ Date: _____

INDEPENDENT PRACTICE

Look at the pictures.
Fill in each blank with A.M. **or** P.M.

Mr. Green takes a walk with
his baby every morning
at 8:45 _____

The lights in the park go
on at 8:05_____

Read and write the time shown on each clock.
Use A.M. **or** P.M. **to show time of the day.**

Josiah wakes up at _____

The July Fourth celebration
ended at _____

5  Brianna eats a snack

at _____

6  Ms. Adams and her children have a picnic

at _____

Fill in each blank with A.M. or P.M.

7 Cooper plays tennis after school at 4:30 _____

8 Adrian does his homework at 8:15 _____ before he goes to bed.

9 Ella leaves home at 7:30 _____ to go to school.

10 Mr. Thomas starts preparing lunch at his restaurant at 10:15 _____

List the times in 7 to 10.
Arrange them in order from the beginning of the day.

11 _____, _____, _____, _____
earliest

3 Bills

Learning Objectives:
- Recognize and identify $1, $5, $10, and $20 bills.
- Exchange money using coins and bills to $20.
- Count money using coins and bills.
- Write amounts of money using $ and ¢.
- Write dollars as cents and cents as dollars.

> **New Vocabulary**
> bills
> dollar ($)
> decimal point

THINK

Jaxon exchanged a twenty-dollar bill for some bills with Hana.
Hana gave Jaxon a five-dollar bill and some other money.
Show in at least three ways the bills and/or coins Jaxon received.

ENGAGE

a   Use  to show a penny, a nickel, a dime, and a quarter.
    Write the value of each coin.

b   Take some bills.
    Are the values of these bills more or less than the coins?

> We use ¢ to represent cents.
> What is another way to
> represent money?

LEARN Recognize the bills and their values

$ means dollars!

A $1 bill has two faces.
It has a value of one dollar or $1.

A $5 bill has two faces.
It has a value of five dollars or $5.

A $10 bill has two faces.
It has a value of ten dollars or $10.

A $20 bill has two faces.
It has a value of twenty dollars or $20.

TRY Practice recognizing the bills and their values

Look at the bills.

Fill in each blank with the number of bills.

1 _____ $1 bills

2 _____ $5 bills

3 _____ $10 bills

4 _____ $20 bills

Write the value of each bill.

5

$_____

6

$_____

7

$_____

8

$_____

ENGAGE

Use to exchange a dime for pennies.
Use  to exchange a ten-dollar bill for one-dollar bills.
What do you notice?
Explain to your partner.

LEARN Exchange and count money

1

 =

1 five-dollar bill

5 one-dollar bills

 =

1 ten-dollar bill   2 five-dollar bills

2 Brandon has some bills.
How much money does Brandon have?
Count on from the greatest value.

20, 30, 40, 50,
60, 65, 66 dollars.

Brandon has $66.

Math Talk

Nolan has a five-dollar bill and 5 one-dollar bills.
Carla has a twenty-dollar bill and a ten-dollar bill.
Lily says that Nolan has 6 bills in all and Carla has 2 bills in all.
So, Nolan has more money than Carla.
Do you agree?
Why?

③  =

1 one-dollar bill   4 quarters

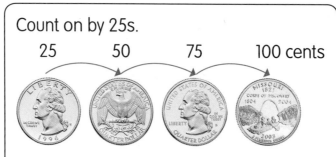

Count on by 25s.

25   50   75   100 cents

Four quarters have a value of 100¢.
100¢ = $1

 =

1 one-dollar bill

10 dimes

Count on by 10s.
10, 20, 30, 40, 50, 60, 70, 80, 90, 100.
Ten dimes have a value of 100¢.

Counting and exchanging money

Work in groups.

(1) Each student to take four bills from a bag of bills.

(2) Count the number of each bill each student takes.
Record in the table below.
An example has been done for you.

Student	Number of one-dollar bills	Number of five-dollar bills	Number of ten-dollar bills	Number of twenty-dollar bills	Total value
A	2	0	1	1	$32

(3) Use to show the amount each student gets in two different ways.

Example:
Student A has a total amount of $32.

Way 1:

Way 2:

Practice exchanging and counting money

Fill in each blank.

1  =

1 twenty-dollar bill   2 _____ bills

2 Max pays for a toy car using the amount below.

The toy car costs $_____.

3 Allison pays for a musical box using the amount below.

The musical box costs $_____.

4  =

1 one-dollar bill   2 _____ and 5 _____

ENGAGE

Use  to show a nickel and three pennies.
How do we write the amount in cents?
Use and to show a five-dollar bill, two quarters, and two pennies.
How do we write the amount in dollars and cents?

LEARN Write an amount of money

1 Hugo has a $5 bill, a quarter, and two dimes.

$5   25¢   10¢   10¢

$5 ⟶ $5.25 ⟶ $5.35 ⟶ $5.45

Hugo has five dollars and forty-five cents.
You write this as $5.45.

> The decimal point is important.
> It separates the cents from
> the dollars.

2 Ryan has two $10 bills and a $5 bill.

He has twenty-five dollars.
Write this amount as $25 or $25.00.

There are no cents.
So, you can write two
zeros after the decimal point.

3 Luke also has some money.

He has twenty-five cents.
Write this amount as 25¢ or $.25.

There are no dollars.
So, you do not write a zero
before the decimal point.

4 You can exchange cents for dollars.

100¢ = $1.00   200¢ = $2.00
                  203¢ = $2.03

Two hundred three cents is two dollars and three cents.

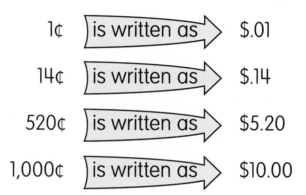

1¢	is written as	$.01
14¢	is written as	$.14
520¢	is written as	$5.20
1,000¢	is written as	$10.00

5 You can exchange dollars for cents.

$1.50 = 150¢

One dollar and fifty cents is one hundred fifty cents.

$7.95	is written as	795¢
$9	is written as	900¢
$.08	is written as	8¢
$.50	is written as	50¢

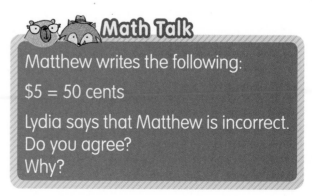

Math Talk

Matthew writes the following:

$5 = 50 cents

Lydia says that Matthew is incorrect.
Do you agree?
Why?

Hands-on Activity Counting and writing amounts of money

Work in pairs.

1 Use 💵 and 🪙 to show your partner these amounts of money.

    a $.80   b $7.00   c $10.66

2 Your partner will show the amounts of money in different ways.

3 You will write the amounts in cents.

    a $.80 = _____ ¢

    b $7.00 = _____ ¢

    c $10.66 = _____ ¢

4 Your partner will check the answers.

5 Trade places.

6 Use 💵 and 🪙 to show your partner these amounts of money.

    a   4¢   b   100¢   c   1,009¢

7 Your partner will show the amounts of money in different ways.

8 You will write the amounts in dollars.

    a   4¢ = $_____

    b   100¢ = $_____

    c   1,009¢ = $_____

9 Your partner will check the answers.

TRY Practice writing an amount of money

Count the money.
Then, write each amount in two different ways.

 1

$_____ or $_____

 2

_____¢ or $_____

3

_____ dollars and _____ cents or $_____

4

_____ dollars and _____ cents or $_____

5

_____ dollars and _____ cents or $_____

Write each amount in cents.

6 $.45 = _____ ¢

7 $2.99 = _____ ¢

8 $3.08 = _____ ¢

9 $4.30 = _____ ¢

Write each amount in dollars.

10 52¢ = $_____

11 675¢ = $_____

12 107¢ = $_____

13 415¢ = $_____

Name: _____   Date: _____

INDEPENDENT PRACTICE

Look at the bills.
Fill in each blank with the number of bills.

1 _____ $1 bills

2 _____ $5 bills

3 _____ $10 bills

4 _____ $20 bills

Write the value of each bill.

5

$_____

6

$_____

7

$_____

8

$_____

Show other ways of exchanging a $20 bill for $1, $5, and $10 bills.

(empty answer box)

Fill in each blank with the amount of money.

$_____

$_____

Show other ways of exchanging a $1 bill for quarters, dimes, nickels, and pennies.

12

Count the money.
Then, write each amount in two different ways.

13

_____ dollars and _____ cents or $_____

14

_____ dollars and _____ cents or $_____

15

_____ dollars and _____ cents or $_____

Fill in each blank.

16 $10.00 = _____ dollars and _____ cents

17 $.80 = _____ dollars and _____ cents

18 $75.02 = _____ dollars and _____ cents

Write each amount in cents.

19 $.12 = _____ ¢

20 $4.99 = _____ ¢

21 $5.00 = _____ ¢

22 $6.03 = _____ ¢

Write each amount in dollars.

23 9¢ = $_____

24 145¢ = $_____

25 230¢ = $_____

26 1,010¢ = $_____

Comparing Amounts of Money

Learning Objectives:
- Compare amounts of money using tables.
- Order amounts of money.

> **New Vocabulary**
> table

**THINK**

The amounts of money are ordered from least to greatest.

$12.91 $21.19 $_____ $30.09

Write a possible amount of money in the blank.

> Which amount of money is the greatest?
> Which amount of money is the least?
> What do I need to find?

ENGAGE

Davi has 4 quarters, 2 dimes, and 3 pennies.
Farrah has 3 quarters, 2 dimes, 3 nickels, and 3 pennies.
Use 🪙 to compare who has more.
How much more?
Explain how you compared.

LEARN Compare amounts of money

1 Mariah has $29.50.
   Simon has $32.20.
   Who has more?

	Dollars	Cents
Mariah	29	50
Simon	32	20

$32.20 is more than $29.50.
$29.50 is less than $32.20.
So, Simon has more money.

You can use a dollars and cents table to compare amounts of money.

First, compare the dollars. $32 is greater than $29.

2 William has $63.25.
   Jasmine has $63.70.
   Who has less?

	Dollars	Cents
William	63	25
Jasmine	63	70

$63.70 is more than $63.25.
$63.25 is less than $63.70.
So, William has less money.

First, compare the dollars. They are equal.
Then, compare the cents. 70¢ is greater than 25¢.

3 Natalie has $40.35.
Emilia has $40.80.
Michael has $44.55.
Who has the greatest amount of money?

	Dollars	Cents
Natalie	40	35
Emilia	40	80
Michael	44	55

$44.55 is the greatest.
$40.35 is the least.
So, Michael has the greatest amount.

From greatest to least, the amounts are:

$44.55 $40.80 $40.35
greatest   least

First, compare the dollars.
$44 is greater than $40.
So, $44.55 is greater than
$40.35 and $40.80.

Next, compare $40.35
and $40.80.

They have equal amount
of dollars.
Then, compare the cents.
80¢ is greater than 35¢.

Math Talk

Hannah writes the following:

$15.40 > $20.25

She says that 40¢ is greater than 25¢.
So, $15.40 is greater than $20.25.
Is she correct?
Why?

TRY Practice comparing amounts of money

Compare the amounts of money.
Fill in each blank with greater than or less than.

1

Dollars	Cents
	95
1	4

$.95 is _____ $1.04.

2

Dollars	Cents
30	50
30	5

$30.50 is _____ $30.05.

Compare the amounts of money.
Answer each question.

Dollars	Cents
50	15
58	45
50	35

3 Which amount is the least? $_____

4 Which amount is the greatest? $_____

Compare and order the amounts of money from least to greatest.

5 $_____ $_____ $_____
        least   greatest

INDEPENDENT PRACTICE

Compare the amounts.
Fill in each blank.

A packet of playing cards costs $5.00.
A kite costs $8.40.

	Dollars	Cents
playing cards	5	00
kite	8	40

1 $_____ is more than $_____.

2 $_____ is less than $_____.

3 Which item costs more? _____

Complete the table.
Compare the amounts.
Then, fill in each blank.

4 Ms. Jackson has $40.60.
Ms. Campbell has $40.55.

	Dollars	Cents
Ms. Jackson		
Ms. Campbell		

5 $_____ is less than $_____.

6 $_____ is more than $_____.

7 Who has less amount of money? _____

8 Mr. Nelson saves $52.08.
Ms. Carter saves $60.72.
Ms. Gomez saves $52.80.

	Dollars	Cents
Mr. Nelson		
Ms. Carter		
Ms. Gomez		

9 Do all of them save the same amount of money? _____

10 $_____ is the greatest amount.

11 $_____ is the least amount.

12 Who saves the least? _____

Compare the amounts.
Answer each question.

$70.03

$70.63

$60.30

Coin Bank A   Coin Bank B   Coin Bank C

13 Which coin bank has the greatest amount of money? _____

14 Which coin bank has the least amount of money? _____

Compare and order the amounts of money from greatest to least.

15 $_____ $_____ $_____
        greatest   least

5 Real-World Problems: Money

Learning Objective:
• Use bar models to solve real-world problems in dollars only or in cents only.

THINK

Harper and Sophie have $1.25 each.
Each of them has a different number of coins.
What are the possible number of coins that each of them have?

ENGAGE

Victor has 75¢.
The amount of money Layla has is less than the amount of money Victor has.
The amount of money Kate has is less than the amount of money Victor has but more than the amount of money Layla has.
Draw a bar model to show the amount of money each child has.

What other strategy can we use to find the answer?

LEARN Solve real-world problems involving money and part-whole models

1 Riley has 27¢.
Her grandmother gives her 15¢ more.
She spends 19¢.
How much money does Riley have left?

STEP 1 Understand the problem.

How much does Riley have?
How much more does her grandmother give to her?
How much does she spend?
What do I need to find?

STEP 2 Think of a plan.
I can draw a bar model to show the parts and whole.

STEP 3 Carry out the plan.

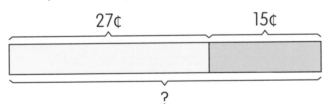

27 + 15 = 42

Riley has 42¢ in all.

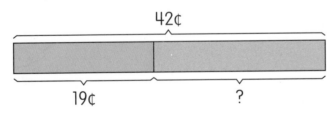

42 − 19 = 23

Riley has 23¢ left.

STEP 4 Check the answer.
I can work backwards.

$23 + 19 = 42$
$42 - 15 = 27$
My answer
is correct.

TRY Practice solving real-world problems involving money and part-whole models

Solve.

Use the bar model to help you.

These are some items on sale.

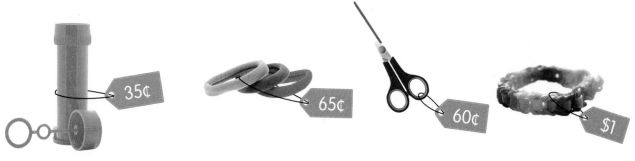

35¢

65¢

60¢

$1

a bottle of
soap bubbles

hair ties

scissors

bracelet

1. Ivan buys the bottle of soap bubbles.
Julia buys the hair ties.
How much do they spend in all?

_____ ◯ _____ = _____

_____ ¢ = $_____

They spend $_____ in all.

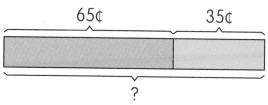

65¢   35¢

?

2 Lauren buys a pair of scissors and a bracelet.
How much does Lauren pay in all?

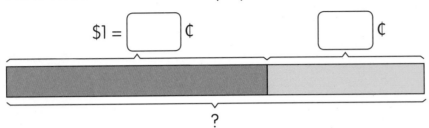

$1 = _____ ¢

_____ ◯ _____ = _____

_____ ¢ = $_____

Lauren pays $_____ in all.

3 Rafael bought an eraser and a marker.
The eraser cost a quarter.
The marker cost 8 dimes.

a How much did Rafael pay in all?

b After paying for the eraser and the marker, Rafael had
2 quarters and 3 dimes left.
How much money did Rafael have in the beginning?

a

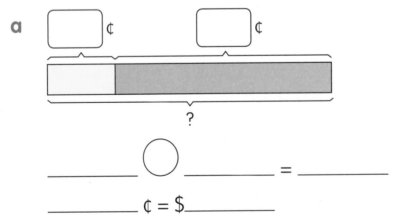

_____ ◯ _____ = _____

_____ ¢ = $_____

Rafael paid $_____ in all.

b

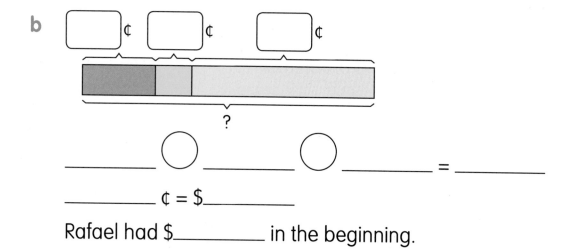

_____ ○ _____ ○ _____ = _____

_____ ¢ = $_____

Rafael had $_____ in the beginning.

4 A stool costs $18.
A table costs $66.
Mr. Morris has $153 at first.
He buys a stool and a table.
How much does Mr. Morris have left?

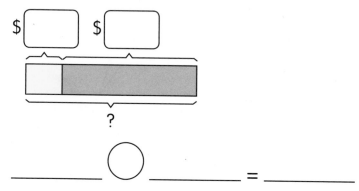

_____ ○ _____ = _____

The stool and the table cost $_____ in all.

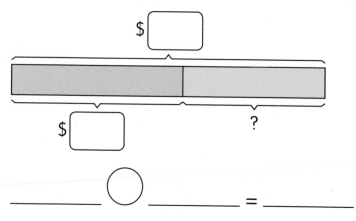

_____ ○ _____ = _____

Mr. Morris has $_____ left.

ENGAGE

Use 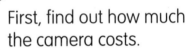 to solve real-world problems.

Sarah has 50¢.

Hayden has 75¢.

How much more money does Hayden have than Sarah?

LEARN Solve real-word problems involving money and comparison models

1. A DVD player costs $168.
A camera costs $75 more than the DVD player.
A computer costs $300.
How much more does the computer cost than the camera?

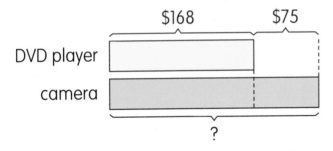

$$168 + 75 = 243$$
The camera costs $243.

First, find out how much the camera costs.

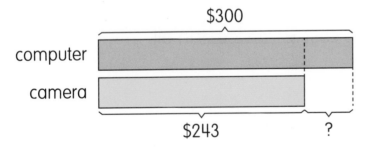

$$300 - 243 = 57$$

The computer costs $57 more than the camera.

Check

$$243 - 75 = 168$$
$$57 + 243 = 300$$

The answer is correct.

Work in groups.

1. Each student will bring a supermarket advertisement.

2. Write a real-world problem using the advertisements for other groups to solve.

3. Use only the items in the advertisements that are in dollars or cents.

| Mr. Moore | more than | altogether |
| less than | buys | Ms. Taylor |

Your real-world problem:

Answer:

TRY Practice solving real-world problems involving money and comparison models

Solve. Use the bar model to help you.

1. A toy train costs $42.
   A toy car costs $38 more.
   A toy airplane costs $99.

   a How much does the toy car cost?

   b How much more does the toy airplane cost than the toy car?

   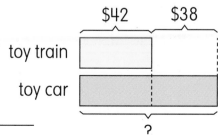

   a _____ ◯ _____ = _____

   The toy car costs $_____.

b

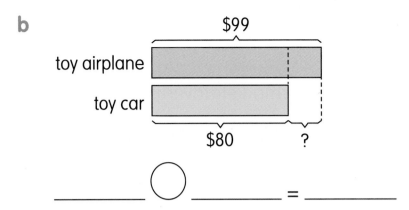

_____ ◯ _____ = _____

The toy airplane costs $_____ more than the toy car.

② Mr. Ward bought a pair of shoes and a pair of boots.
He paid $24 for the pair of shoes.
He paid $32 more for the pair of boots than for the pair of shoes.
After paying for the pair of shoes and the pair of boots,
Mr. Ward had $45 left.
How much did Mr. Ward have in the beginning?

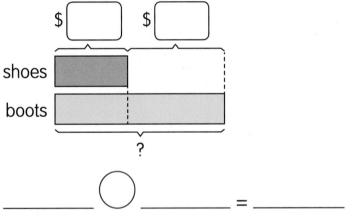

_____ ◯ _____ = _____

Mr. Ward paid $_____ for the pair of boots.

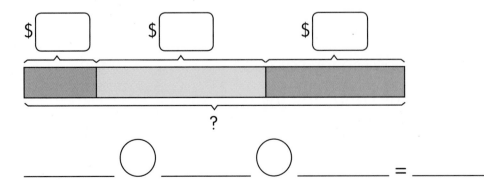

_____ ◯ _____ ◯ _____ = _____

Mr. Ward had $_____ in the beginning.

INDEPENDENT PRACTICE

Solve.
Use the bar model to help you.

1 Anthony buys an apple for 35¢.
Molly buys a lemon for 82¢.
How much do they spend in all?

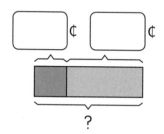

2 A notepad costs 80¢.
A sticker costs 25¢.
After buying one of each item, Paula has 35¢ left.
How much money does she have at first?

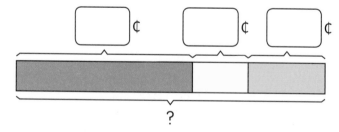

Solve.

Draw a bar model to help you.

3 Ms. Kelly and Mr. Cook have $230.
Ms. Kelly has $159.
How much money does Mr. Cook have?

4 Clara bought a pencil for 25¢ and an eraser for 15¢.
If she had 81¢ at first, how much money did she have left?

5 Stella has a dollar bill and 2 quarters in her purse.
She buys some candy for 55¢.
How much does she have left?

6 Mr. Martinez has a five-dollar bill.
He wants to buy a slice of cake and a cream roll.
The slice of cake costs $6 and the cream roll costs 45¢.
How much more money does he need?

7 Bag A costs $700.
It costs $265 more than Bag B.
Bag C costs $309.
How much more does Bag B cost than Bag C?

8 Ms. Cox has $450 in the bank.
She has $18 less than Ms. Ramos.
Ms. Ramos spends $226.
How much money does Ms. Ramos have left?

9 Joshua has 95¢.
He has 20¢ more than his sister.
How much money do Joshua and his sister have in all?

Name: _____ Date: _____

Mathematical Habit **3** **Construct viable arguments**

a Look at the time shown on the clock.
Rebeca wrote the time incorrectly.
Spot the mistake.
Then, fill in the blank with the correct time.

Rebeca wrote: The time is 5:45.

The correct time is _____.

b She drew the hour and minute hands on the clock to show 7:55.
This was what she drew.

Spot the mistake.
Then, draw the hour and minute hands on the clock to show 7:55.

The correct way is 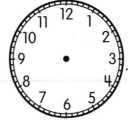.

Mathematical Habit 4 Model with mathematics

Leah has the following amount of money.

She wants to buy the doll shown below.

$15

Leah says that she does not have enough money to buy the doll.
How much more money does she need?
Draw a bar model to help you.

Problem Solving with Heuristics

1 **Mathematical Habit 1** Persevere in solving problems

Maya completed her homework at 5:35 P.M.

She started doing her homework 1 hour earlier.

She reached home 25 minutes before she started on her homework.

Maya reached home at _____.

2 | **Mathematical Habit 1** | **Persevere in solving problems**

Mason saves his money in $1 bills and quarters.
So far he has saved $5.
He has more than 2 bills and more than 4 coins.
How many $1 bills and quarters does Mason have?

Make a list to help you!

CHAPTER WRAP-UP

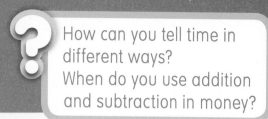

? How can you tell time in different ways?
When do you use addition and subtraction in money?

Time

Reading and Writing Time

Using A.M. and P.M.

Skip count by 5s to tell the time.

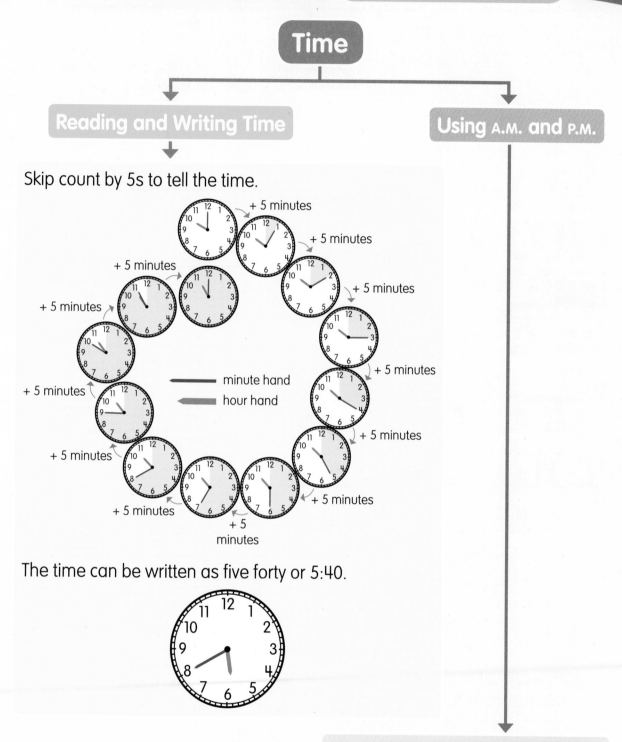

minute hand
hour hand

The time can be written as five forty or 5:40.

A.M. is used to talk about time just after midnight to just before noon.

P.M. is used to talk about time just after noon to just before midnight.

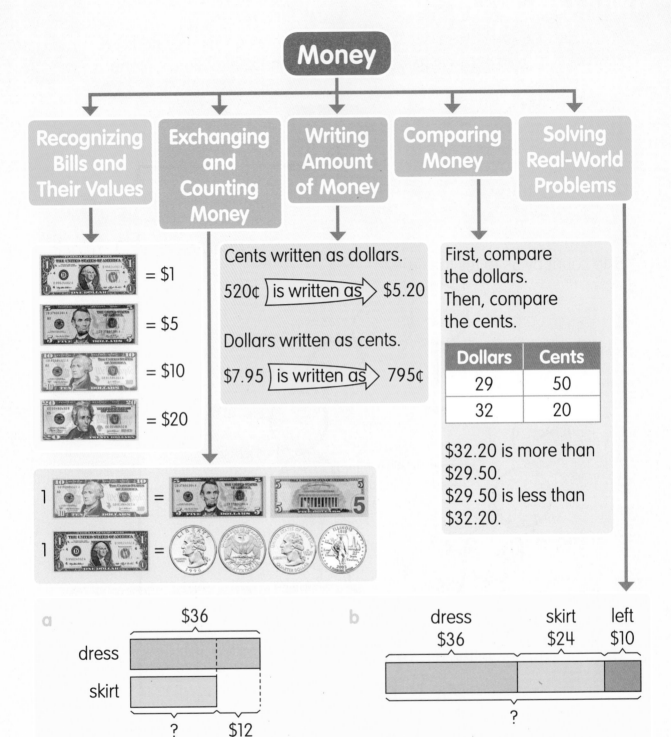

Money

Recognizing Bills and Their Values

= $1

= $5

= $10

= $20

Exchanging and Counting Money

1 [$10] = [$5] [$5]

1 [$1] = (4 quarters)

Writing Amount of Money

Cents written as dollars.

520¢ is written as $5.20

Dollars written as cents.

$7.95 is written as 795¢

Comparing Money

First, compare the dollars. Then, compare the cents.

Dollars	Cents
29	50
32	20

$32.20 is more than $29.50.
$29.50 is less than $32.20.

Solving Real-World Problems

a

$36

dress

skirt

? $12

36 − 12 = 24
The skirt costs $24.

b

dress $36   skirt $24   left $10

?

36 + 24 + 10 = 70
She has $70 at first.

Name: _____ Date: _____

Fill in each blank.
Skip count by 5s to help you.

 **1** _____ minutes later ⟶

9 o'clock   _____ minutes after 9 o'clock

Draw the minute hand on the clock to show the time.

2   9:45   **3**   3:20

Write each time.

4    **5**

_____   _____

6  `9:25`   **7**  `3:00`

_____   _____

Look at the pictures.
Fill in each blank with A.M. or P.M.

8

Alex and Ellie went for a late-night movie at 11:50 _____

They returned home at 1:30 _____

9

Manuel went to the library 1 hour after 12:00 noon.

The time was 1:00 _____

Arrange the times in order from the beginning of the day.

10 | 11:50 P.M. | 1:30 A.M. | 12 noon | 1:00 P.M |

_____, _____, _____, _____
   earliest

Look at the bills.
Fill in each blank with the number of bills.

11 _____ $1 bill

12 _____ $5 bills

13 _____ $10 bills

14 _____ $20 bills

Write the value of each bill.

15

$_____

16

$_____

17

$_____

18

$_____

Show other ways of exchanging a $20 bill for $1 and $5 bills.

19

Fill in the blank with the amount of money.

20

$_____

Show other ways of exchanging a $1 bill for dimes and nickels.

21

Write each amount in dollars or cents.

22 $7.00 = _____ ¢

23 $.85 = _____ ¢

24 $.06 = _____ ¢

25 910¢ = $_____

26 55¢ = $_____

27 10¢ = $_____

Count the amount of money in each set.
Compare and order the amounts of money from greatest to least.

28

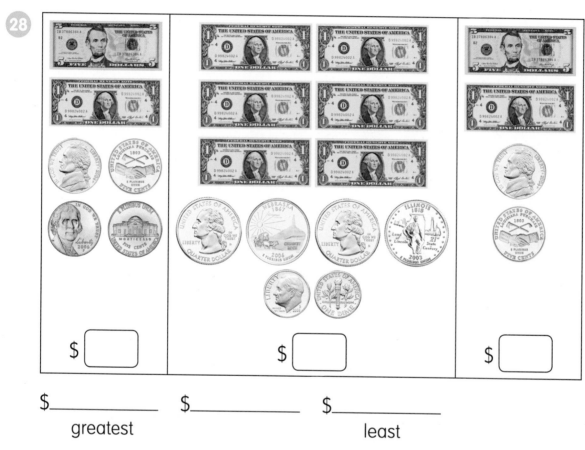

$ [   ] $ [   ] $ [   ]

$_____ $_____ $_____
    greatest   least

Compare the amounts of money. Answer each question.

$62.90 $69.00 $62.35

29 Which is the least amount? $_____

30 Which is the greatest amount? $_____

Compare and order the amounts of money from least to greatest.

31 $_____ $_____ $_____
        least   greatest

Solve.
Draw a bar model to help you.

32 Jacob has a $1 bill.
He buys an eraser that costs 30¢.
He also buys a ruler that costs 50¢.
How much change will he receive?

33 Mr. Murphy has $330.
He has $79 less than Ms. Rogers.
Ms. Rogers spends $62.
How much does Ms. Rogers have now?

Assessment Prep

**Look at the time on each clock.
Answer the question.**

Clock A

Clock B

Clock C

Clock D

34 Which clock shows 3:15? _____

Compare and order the amounts of money from greatest to least.

$80.40 $84.04 $80.04

35 $_____ $_____ $_____

greatest   least

Name: _____   Date: _____

In a Sports Shop

1 Mr. Mitchell has the bill shown.
Write the amount.

$ _____

Circle the bills and coins to make the above amount.

2 Mr. Mitchell receives a change of $3.39 after paying for some items.
Draw bills and coins to show the amount.

3 The next morning, the Mitchell family wake up at 7:45.
   Draw the minute hand and the hour hand to show the time.

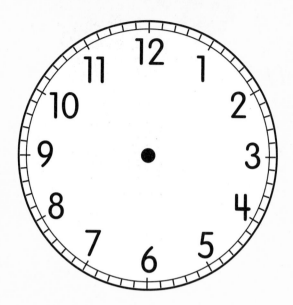

4 What would you be doing at 7:45 A.M.?

5 What would you be doing at 7:45 P.M.?

6 Amir starts to eat breakfast at 8:40 _____ (A.M. or P.M.)

7 Draw the minute hand and the hour hand to show 8:40.

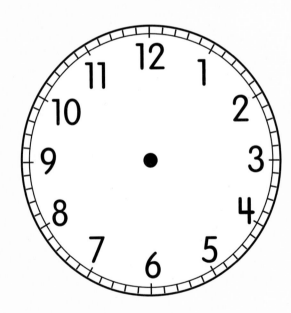

8 Mr. Mitchell makes a campfire at 8:15 _____ (A.M. or P.M.)

9 Draw the minute hand and the hour hand to show 8:15.

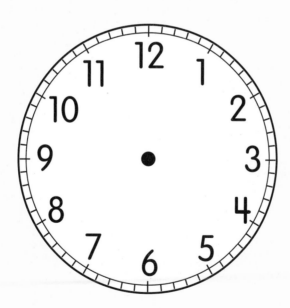

Rubric

Point(s)	Level	My Performance
7–8	4	• Most of my answers are correct. • I show all my work correctly. • I explain my thinking clearly and completely.
5–6.5	3	• Some of my answers are correct. • I show some of my work correctly. • I explain my thinking clearly.
3–4.5	2	• A few of my answers are correct. • I show little work correctly. • I explain some of my thinking clearly.
0–2.5	1	• A few of my answers are correct. • I show little or no work. • I do not explain my thinking clearly.

Teacher's Comments

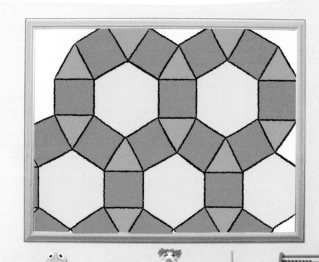

I use solid shapes to make this castle.

I use lines and curves to draw this picture.

How can you make figures using flat shapes and models using solid shapes?

Name: _____   Date: _____

Identifying flat shapes

a

square

rectangle

triangle

circle

trapezoid

hexagon

b

rectangle

triangle

circle

square

▶ **Quick Check**

Name each shape.

1

2

3

_____   _____   _____

Look at the pictures.
Name each flat shape you see.

4

5

6

_____   _____   _____

Identifying sides and corners in flat shapes

Some flat shapes have sides and corners.

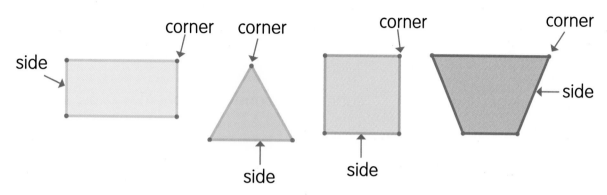

Some flat shapes do not have sides and corners.

▶ **Quick Check**

Count the number of sides and corners in each shape.

7

_____ sides

_____ corners

8

_____ sides

_____ corners

9
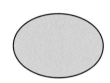

_____ sides

_____ corners

10

_____ sides

_____ corners

11

_____ sides

_____ corners

12

_____ sides

_____ corners

Identifying solid shapes

a

rectangular prism   cylinder   cube   cone   sphere   pyramid

b

sphere   rectangular prism   cone

▶ **Quick Check**

Name each solid shape.

13   14   15

_____   _____   _____

Look at the pictures.
Name each solid shape you see.

16    17    18

_____   _____   _____

Name: _____   Date: _____

Lines and Surfaces

Learning Objectives:
- Recognize, identify, and describe lines and curves.
- Draw lines and curves.
- Identify, classify, and count flat and curved surfaces.
- Identify solids that can stack, slide, and/or roll.

New Vocabulary
line
curve

THINK

Eva says that a curve is made up of many lines.
Is she correct? Why?
How can you show that curves are special types of lines?
Talk about it with your partner.

ENGAGE

a   Look at the three shapes shown below.

Compare the shapes.
How are they the same?
How are they different?
Share with your partner.

b   Draw a new shape.
Share with your partner the lines you used.

LEARN Recognize and identify lines and curves

1 Martin uses a pencil and a ruler to draw a line.

These are also lines.

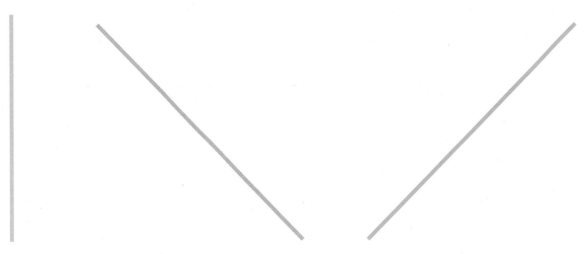

2 Next, Martin draws a curve.

These are also curves.

Hands-on Activity Drawing lines and curves

Work in small groups.

(1) Your teacher will give you these solids.

rectangular prism   cylinder

(2) Use the rectangular prism to draw two different lines.

(3) Use the cylinder to draw two different curves.

(4) Share your drawings with your classmates.

(5) a   What other solid shapes can you draw with lines?

_____

b   What other solid shapes can you draw with curves?

_____

TRY Practice recognizing and identifying lines and curves

Look at the drawings.
Answer each question.

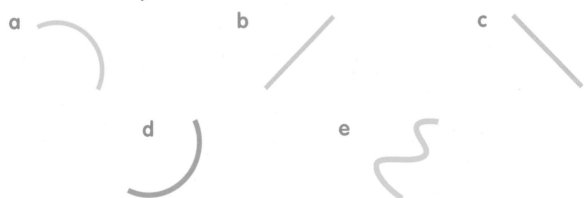

a   b   c

d   e

① Which are lines? _____

② Which are curves? _____

Look at the drawings.
Circle the lines.
Then, make a ✗ on the curves.

③

Look at the picture.

How many lines are there?
How many curves are there?
How do you know?
Talk about it with your partner.

LEARN Use lines and curves to make shapes

① Owen uses lines and curves to draw a flower.

Owen uses 10 lines and 10 curves.

Hands-on Activity Using lines and curves to make shapes

① Draw a shape with 2 lines and a curve.

Example:

② Draw a shape with these lines and curves.

a 2 curves and a line

b More than 2 lines and more than 2 curves

③ a How many lines did you use in ② b? _____

b How many curves did you use ② b? _____

TRY Practice using lines and curves to make shapes

Each picture is made with lines and curves.
Fill in each blank.

1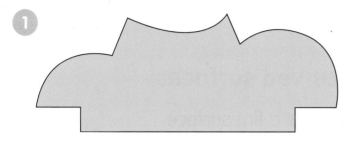

_____ lines

_____ curves

2

_____ lines

_____ curves

3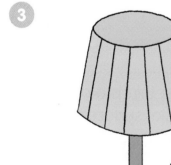

_____ lines

_____ curves

ENGAGE

Take two different .
Can you stack, slide, or roll each solid?
Tell your classmates why.

LEARN Identify flat and curved surfaces

1 The top of your teacher's desk has a flat surface.

Move your hand over the top of the desk.
Does your hand turn?

> What other things around you have flat surfaces?

2 This ball does not have a flat surface.
It has a curved surface.
Move your hand over the surface of a ball.
Does your hand turn?

What other things around
you have curved surfaces?

3 These objects have flat surfaces.

flat surfaces

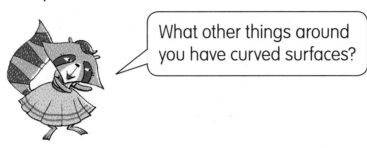

flat surfaces

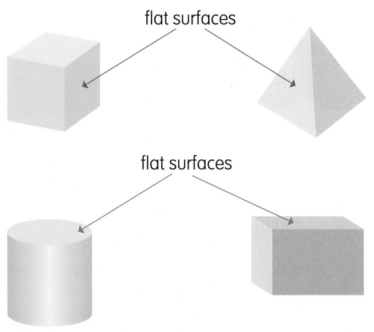

You can slide objects that have a flat surface.
You can stack some objects that have more than one
flat surface.

4 These objects have curved surfaces.

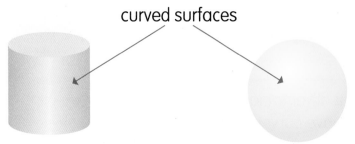

curved surfaces

curved surface

You can roll objects that have curved surfaces.

Math Talk

Think of an object that you can slide and roll.
How many flat surfaces does it have?
How about curved surfaces?
Talk about it with your partner.

TRY Practice identifying flat and curved surfaces

Look at the pictures.
Answer each question.

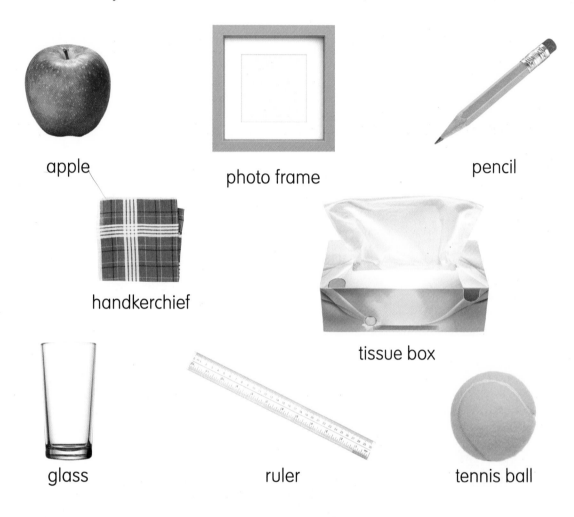

apple

photo frame

pencil

handkerchief

tissue box

glass

ruler

tennis ball

1 Which objects have only flat surfaces?

_____

2 Which objects have only curved surfaces?

_____

3 Which objects have flat and curved surfaces?

_____

Look at the pictures.
Fill in each blank with flat or curved.

4

This is a box.
It can slide.
Why?
It has _____ surfaces.

5

This is a ball.
It can roll.
Why?
It has a _____ surface.

6

You can stack, slide, or roll this container.
Why?
It has _____ and _____
surfaces.

7

You can slide or roll this cone.
Why?
It has _____ and _____
surfaces.

INDEPENDENT PRACTICE

Color shapes with only lines blue.
Color shapes with only curves green.
Color shapes with lines and curves yellow.

 1

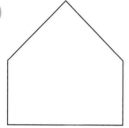 

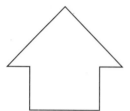   

Count the lines and curves in each picture.
Fill in each blank.

2

There are _____ lines and _____ curves.

③

There are _____ lines and _____ curves.

Draw a shape with less than 6 lines.

④

Draw a shape with more than 4 curves.

⑤

Draw a shape with more than 8 lines and curves.

6

Look at the pictures.
Complete the table.

7

party hat   flask   box   watermelon

Object	Number of Flat Surfaces	Number of Curved Surfaces
Party hat		
Flask		
Box		
Watermelon		

Look at the pictures.
Answer each question.

cube   cone   orange   book

8 Which objects have flat surfaces?

_____

9 Which objects have curved surfaces?

_____

10 Which objects can you slide?

_____

11 Which objects can you stack?

_____

12 Which objects can you roll?

_____

13 Which objects can you slide and roll?

_____

Name: _____ Date: _____

Flat Shapes

Learning Objectives:
- Recognize and identify flat shapes.
- Cut flat shapes into equal parts.
- Use halves, thirds, and fourths to describe equal parts.
- Recognize that equal parts of the same whole do not need to have the same shape.
- Combine flat shapes and take apart figures.
- Recognize and draw shapes with a given number of angles.
- Draw shapes and figures on dot paper and square grid paper.

New Vocabulary
quadrilateral
pentagon
equal parts
third of
thirds
figure
angles

 **THINK**

A hexagon is a flat shape.
It can be cut into other flat shapes.
Draw lines on each hexagon to cut it into other flat shapes.
Show three different ways.

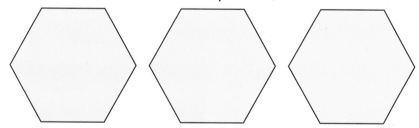

ENGAGE

Take some .

Talk to your classmates about the shapes you took.
How can you group the shapes?
Share your ideas with your classmates.

LEARN Identify more flat shapes

1 These are flat shapes you know.

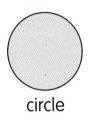 circle

 triangle

 square

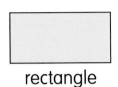 rectangle

 trapezoid

 hexagon

2 These are quadrilaterals.

 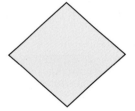

A quadrilateral has four sides.
Rectangles and squares are
also quadrilaterals.

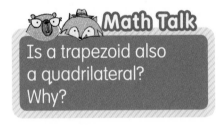

Math Talk

Is a trapezoid also
a quadrilateral?
Why?

3 This is a pentagon.

A pentagon has five sides.

Work in pairs.

Activity 1 Identifying flat shapes

(1) Look at the things around you.
Make a list of the things that have flat shapes.

Flat Shapes	Things Around You
○	
△	
▭	
▭	
⬯	
⬡	

Activity 2 Making patterns with flat shapes

(1) Your teacher will give you a set of shape cut-outs.
Color and cut out the shapes.

(2) Arrange the cut-outs to make three different patterns.
Glue each pattern on a piece of paper.

③ How many shapes did you use to make each pattern?
What are the patterns that you made?

④ Share your pattern with your class.

TRY Practice identifying more flat shapes

Look at the picture.
Complete the table.

①

Flat Shape	Number of Flat Shapes
Triangle	
Rectangle	
Square	
Circle	
Pentagon	

Mathematical Habit 3 Construct viable arguments

Taylor compares the two flat shapes.
She writes how the two shapes are
alike and different below.

Alike: They are blue.
Different: They have different number of sides.

Do you agree?
Talk with your partner about other ways to tell how the shapes are
alike or different.

ENGAGE

Draw lines to cut the rectangle into 2 equal parts.
How many ways can you cut it into 2 equal parts?
Share your ideas with your partner.

LEARN Combine and cut flat shapes

1 You can combine smaller shapes to make larger shapes.

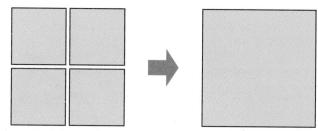

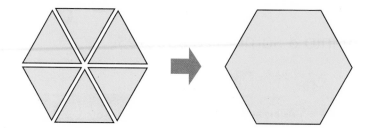

2 You can cut larger shapes into smaller shapes.

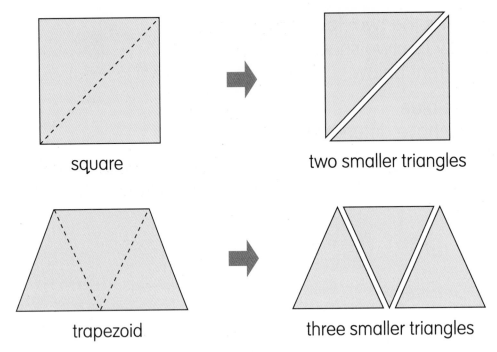

square → two smaller triangles

trapezoid → three smaller triangles

3 You can cut a rectangle into same-size squares.

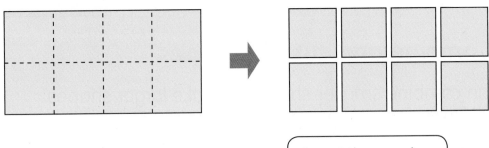

Count the number of squares.

The rectangle can be cut into 8 same-size squares.

Math Talk

How can you cut the rectangle into same-size squares in another way?

4 You can cut shapes into equal parts.

Each shape is cut into 2 equal parts.

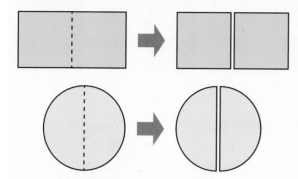

Each part is one half of the rectangle.

Each part is one half of the circle.

Two equal parts, or two halves, make one whole.

Each shape is cut into 3 equal parts.

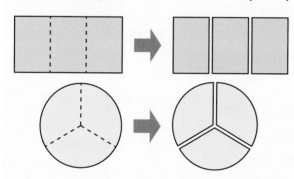

Each part is one third of the rectangle.

Each part is one third of the circle.

Three equal parts, or three thirds, make one whole.

Each shape is cut into 4 equal parts.

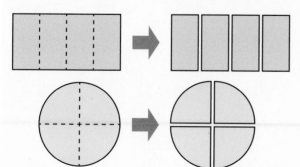

Each part is one fourth of the rectangle.

Each part is one fourth of the circle.

Four equal parts, or four fourths, make one whole.

5 You can cut shapes into equal parts in different ways.

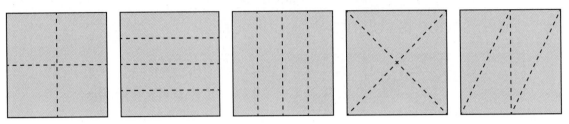

The squares are of the same size.
The equal parts of the squares do
not need to have the same shape.

TRY Practice combining and cutting flat shapes

Complete the table.

1 Trace and cut out 6 small rectangles.
Combine them to make Shape A.
Then, combine them to make Shape B.

Shape A	Shape B

Look at the rectangle.
Fill in each blank.

2 Uriah wants to cover the rectangle with same-size squares.
   He places some squares on the rectangle.

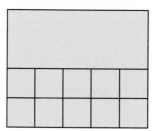

He needs _____ same-size squares to cover the
whole rectangle.

Fill in each blank with halves, thirds, or fourths.

3

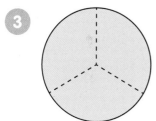

The circle is cut into _____.

4

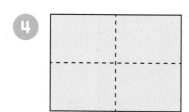

The rectangle is cut into _____.

Draw lines to cut each rectangle into fourths.
Show four different ways.

5

Use 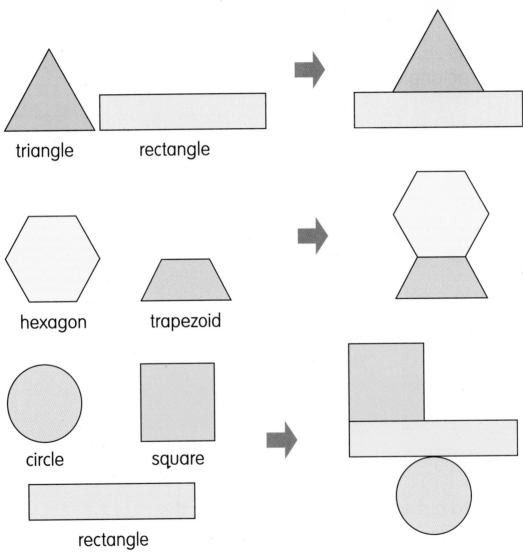 to make a figure of a house.
What shapes did you use?
Share your figure with your classmates.

LEARN Combine shapes and take apart figures

1 You can combine flat shapes to make different figures.

triangle   rectangle

hexagon   trapezoid

circle   square

rectangle

2 This figure is made up of three shapes.

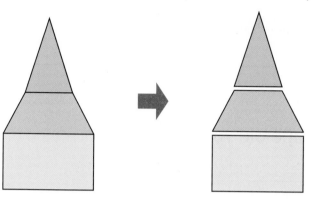

Take apart the figure to see the shapes that make it up.

It is made up of a triangle, a trapezoid, and a rectangle.

Hands-on Activity Using shapes to make figures

Work in groups.

Mathematical Habit 4 Model with mathematics

1. Trace four sets of these shapes.
   Color and cut out the shapes.

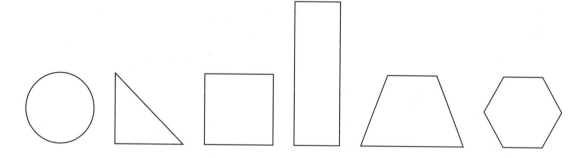

2. Use the cut-outs to make each figure.

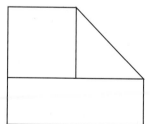 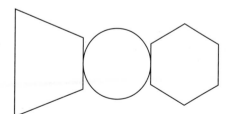

(3) Use the rest of the cut-outs to make other figures.

    a   How many different shapes did you use for each figure?

_____

_____

    b   How many of each shape did you use?

_____

_____

TRY Practice combining shapes and taking apart figures

Name and count each flat shape in the picture.
Complete the table.

Flat Shape	Number of Flat Shapes
Circle	

Draw lines to show the shapes that make up each figure. Write the names of the shapes.

2

_____

3

_____

4

_____

5

_____

Draw a square on dot paper.
Tell your partner how you drew the square.
Draw two other shapes on dot paper.
Share the drawings with your partner.

LEARN Draw figures on dot paper or square grid paper

1. A triangle has 3 corners.
   It has 3 angles.

   A rectangle has 4 corners.
   It has 4 angles.

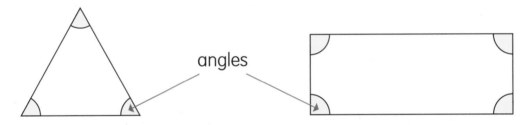

angles

2. You can draw a triangle and a rectangle on dot paper.

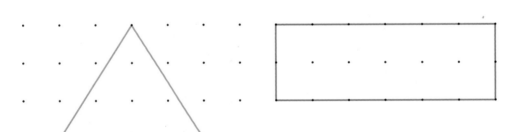

Each corner is at a dot.
Draw the figures by joining the dots.

These are more figures drawn on dot paper.

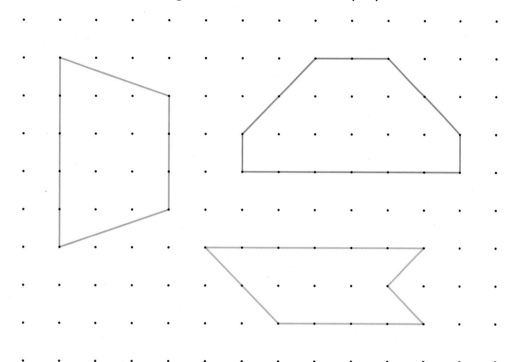

3 You can also draw figures on square grid paper.

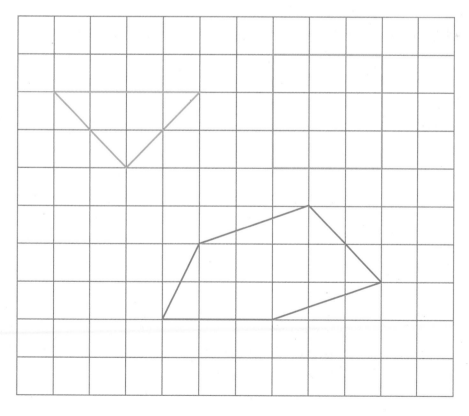

Hands-on Activity Drawing figures on dot paper

Work in pairs.

1 Your teacher will give you a piece of dot paper.

2 Choose 3 dots on the dot grid.
Join the dots to draw a shape.

Example:

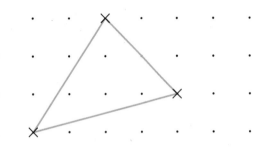

The 3 dots should not all lie on the same line.

What shape did you draw? _____

How many sides does the shape have? _____

3 Repeat ②, this time choosing 4 dots.

What shape did you draw? _____

How many sides does the shape have? _____

4 Repeat ②, this time choosing 5 dots.

What shape did you draw? _____

How many sides does the shape have? _____

5 What do you notice about the number of dots and the number of sides?

_____

Practice drawing figures on dot paper or square grid paper

Fill in each blank.

1

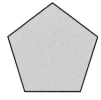

A square has _____ angles.

2

A pentagon has _____ angles.

Copy each figure.
Use the space on the right.

3

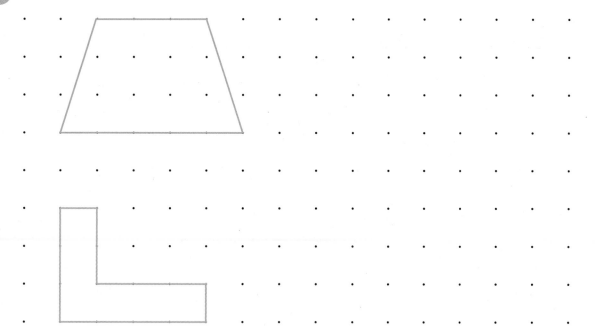

Copy each figure.
Use the space on the right.
Then, fill in each blank.

4

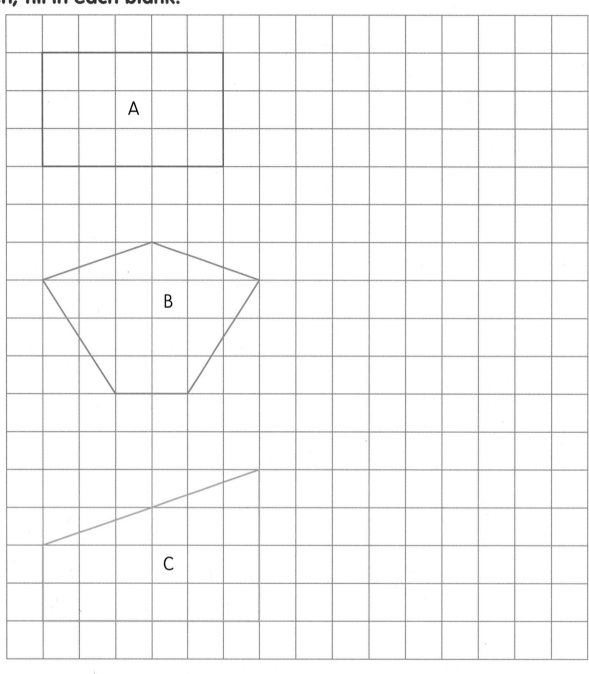

How many angles are there in each figure?

a   Figure A: _____   b   Figure B: _____   c   Figure C: _____

INDEPENDENT PRACTICE

Color the quadrilaterals blue.
Color the pentagons green.

1

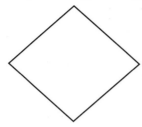

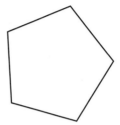
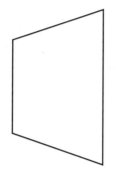
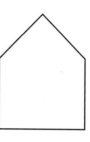

Look at the picture.
Complete the table.

2

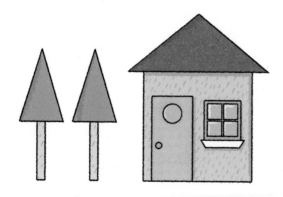

Flat Shape	Number of Flat Shapes
Triangle	
Rectangle	
Square	
Trapezoid	
Circle	

Find the number of squares that make up each rectangle.
Fill in each blank.

 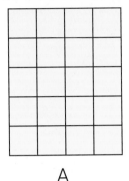

A

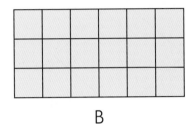

B

a   _____ same-size squares make up rectangle A.

b   _____ same-size squares make up rectangle B.

 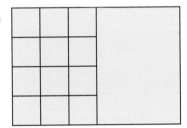

_____ same-size squares make up the whole rectangle.

Fill in each blank.

 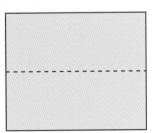

The rectangle is cut into _____ equal parts.

Each part is one _____ of the rectangle.

_____ halves make a whole.

6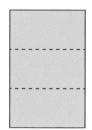

The circle is cut into _____ equal parts.

Each part is one _____ of the circle.

_____ fourths make a whole.

7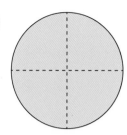

The rectangle is cut into _____ equal parts.

Each part is one _____ of the rectangle.

_____ thirds make a whole.

Put a ✗ on the incorrect shape(s).

8 4 fourths

   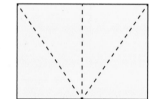

9 3 thirds

 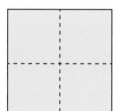 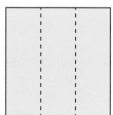 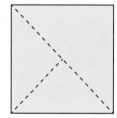

10 2 halves

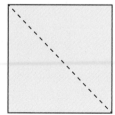 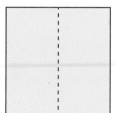  

Use these shapes to draw a figure.

Draw lines to show the shapes that make up the figure.
Write the names of the shapes.

It is made up of _____

_____.

Copy each figure.
Use the space on the right.

13

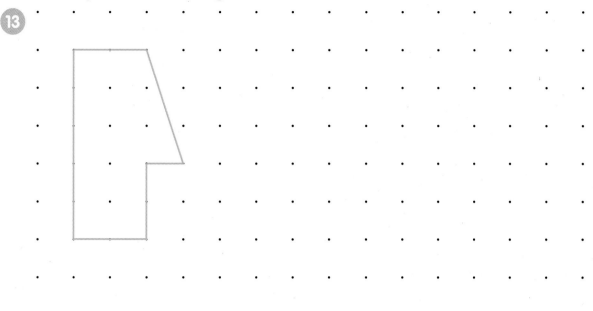

14

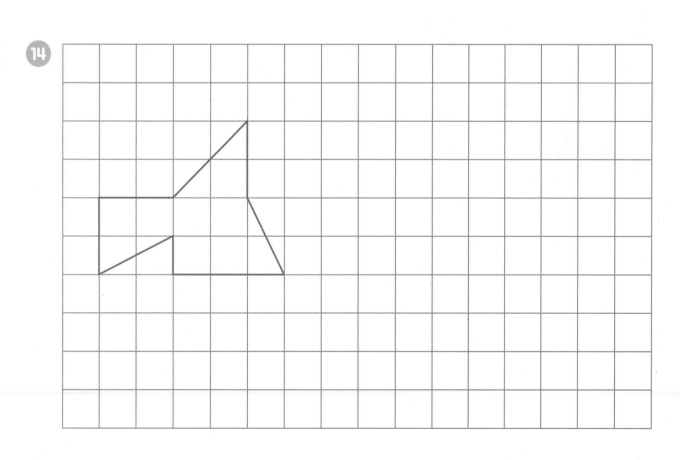

Draw a quadrilateral.
Circle the angles.

Draw a shape with 5 angles.

16

© 2020 Marshall Cavendish Education Pte Ltd

3 Solid Shapes

Learning Objectives:
- Recognize and identify solid shapes.
- Make models using solid shapes.
- Combine solid shapes and take apart models.
- Identify and count the equal faces on a cube.
- Draw a cube on dot paper.

New Vocabulary
face

 **THINK**

Look at the shape below.

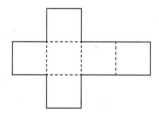

Trace the flat shape on a piece of paper.
Then, cut it out.
Fold along the dotted lines to form a solid shape.
What is the solid shape?

ENGAGE

Use to make a model with your classmates.
How many of each did you use?

LEARN Use solid shapes to make models

1 Look at these solid shapes.

cube   rectangular   cone   cylinder   pyramid   sphere
           prism

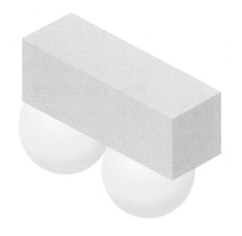

I can make a model using a rectangular prism and 2 spheres.

I can make a model using a cone and a cylinder.

I can make a model using a pyramid and a cube.

2 This model is made of three different solid shapes.

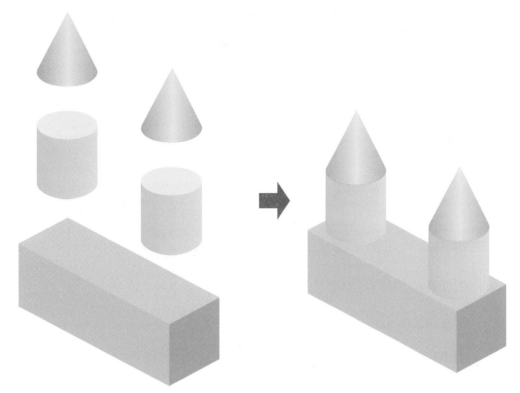

I can make this model using 2 cones, 2 cylinders, and a rectangular prism.

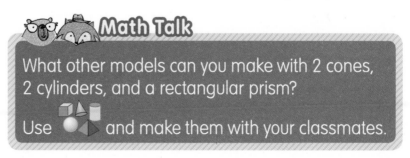

Math Talk

What other models can you make with 2 cones, 2 cylinders, and a rectangular prism?

Use ⬛🔺🔵◀ and make them with your classmates.

Hands-on Activity Using solid shapes to make models

Work in small groups.

(1) Use these solid shapes.

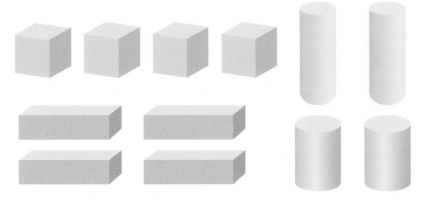

Make a model using

a   any four solid shapes.

b   at least two solid shapes of each type.

(2) Use two sets of these.

a   Use at least six of the solid shapes to make a model.

b   Ask your classmates to list the solid shapes in your model.

(3) Trade places. Repeat (2) a and (2) b.

TRY Practice using solid shapes to make models

Circle the solid shapes that make up each model.

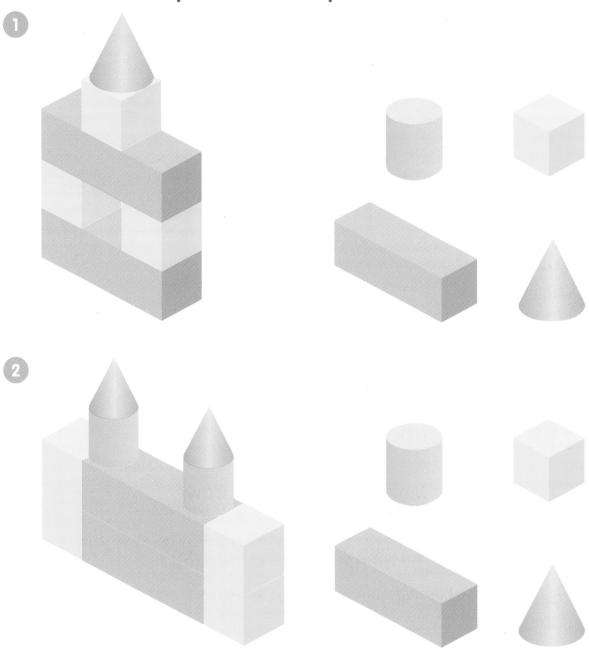

1

2

Count the solid shapes in the model.
Complete the table.

③

Solid Shape	Number of Solid Shapes
Cube	
Rectangular prism	
Cylinder	
Cone	
Sphere	

ENGAGE

Take a cube.
How many flat surfaces does it have?
What do you notice about each flat surface?
Talk about it with your partner.

LEARN Draw a cube on dot paper

Hands-on Activity Making a cube with straws

Work in groups.

Mathematical Habit 4 Use mathematical models

① Your teacher will give you 12 straws and some clay.

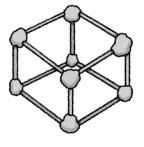

② First, use four straws to make a square.

③ Then, use the rest of the straws to make a cube.

© 2020 Marshall Cavendish Education Pte Ltd

1 Each flat surface of a solid is called a face.

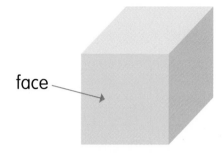

face

A cube has 6 faces.
Each face is a square.

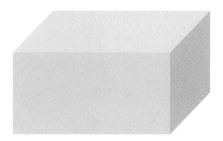

A rectangular prism also has 6 faces.

What is the shape of each face of the rectangular prism?

Math Talk

How is a rectangular prism different from a cube?
Talk about it with your partner.

2 You can draw a cube on dot paper.

STEP 1 Draw a square.

STEP 2 Draw another square.

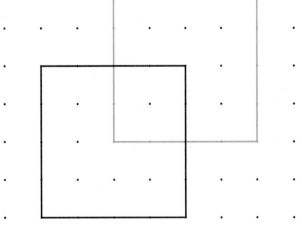

Draw lines to join the corners of the squares.

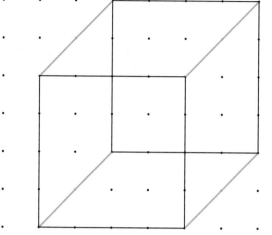

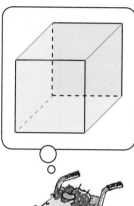

STEP 4 You can only see three faces from this view.
Erase the lines inside the cube to show three faces.

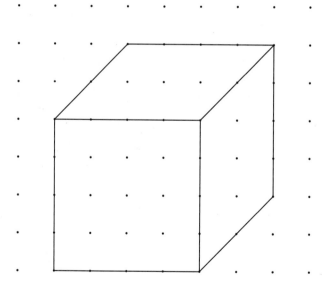

You can also use dotted
lines to show the faces
that you cannot see.

3 You can draw a cube in another way.

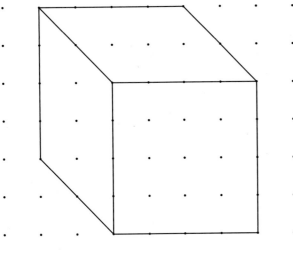

TRY Practice drawing a cube on dot paper

Color the shapes to show all the faces of the solid shape.

1

Draw two different cubes on the dot paper.

2

Work in groups of two or three.

1 Use some  so that they make a rectangle.

 a What shapes do you use?

 b How many of each shape do you use?

 c Show two other ways to make a rectangle.

2 Look around your school.
 Find two objects that have these solid shapes.

 a cube

 b cone

 c rectangular prism

 d cylinder

 e sphere

Example:

The tissue box is a rectangular prism.

Name: _____   Date: _____

INDEPENDENT PRACTICE

Count the solid shapes in the model.
Complete the table.

①

Solid Shape	Number of Solid Shapes
Cube	
Rectangular prism	
Cylinder	

Circle the solid shapes that make up the model.

②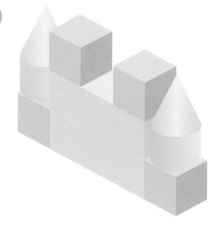

Color the flat shape(s) that is a face of the solid.

3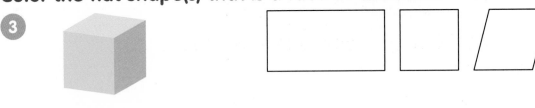

4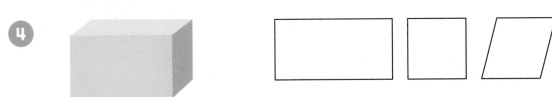

Draw two different cubes on the dot paper.

5

Name: _____ Date: _____

Mathematical Habit 3 | Construct viable arguments

Jordan put the following shapes into three groups.

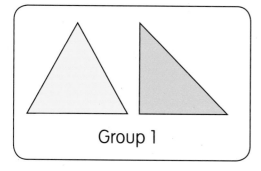

Group 1

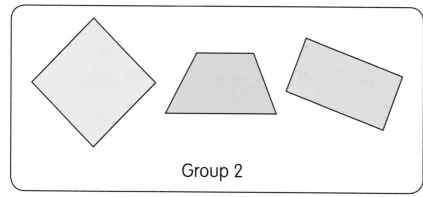

Group 2

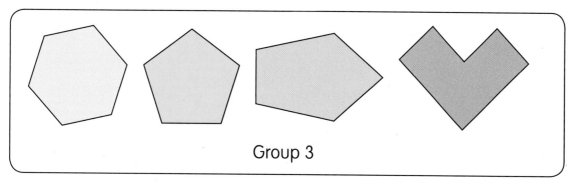

Group 3

How did she group the shapes?

_____

_____

_____

_____

_____

Problem Solving with Heuristics

1 **Mathematical Habit 1** **Persevere in solving problems**

Look at the figure.
How many lines and curves are there?

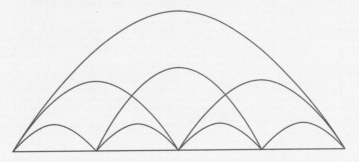

There are _____ curves and _____ line.

2 **Mathematical Habit 1** **Persevere in solving problems**

Trace and cut out the shapes to make a square.

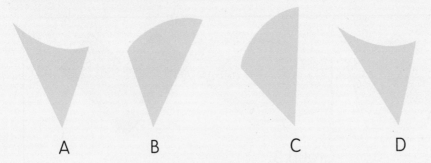

A   B   C   D

© 2020 Marshall Cavendish Education Pte Ltd

3 | **Mathematical Habit** | **1** | **Persevere in solving problems**

This is a tangram.
It is a square made up of seven different pieces.

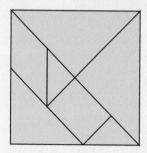

Make a copy of this tangram.
Then, cut along the lines like this:

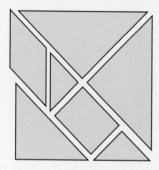

Mix up the pieces.
Then, put them back in another way into the shape of a square.

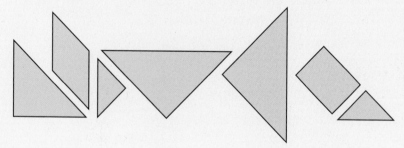

4 **Mathematical Habit** **2** **Use mathematical reasoning**

Ms. Ruiz buys two waffles of the same size.
She cuts one of the waffles into fourths.
Then, she gives a piece of the waffle to Renata.
She cuts the other waffle into thirds.
Then, she gives a piece of the waffle to Colton.
Who gets a bigger piece of waffle?
Draw models to explain your answer.

CHAPTER WRAP-UP

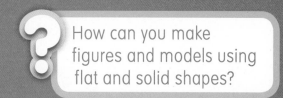

? How can you make figures and models using flat and solid shapes?

Lines and Surfaces

Identifying Lines and Curves

lines

curves

Making Shapes

You can use lines and curves to make shapes.

Identifying Flat and Curved Surfaces

Objects with flat surface can be

stacked

moved by sliding

Objects with curved surface can be

moved by rolling

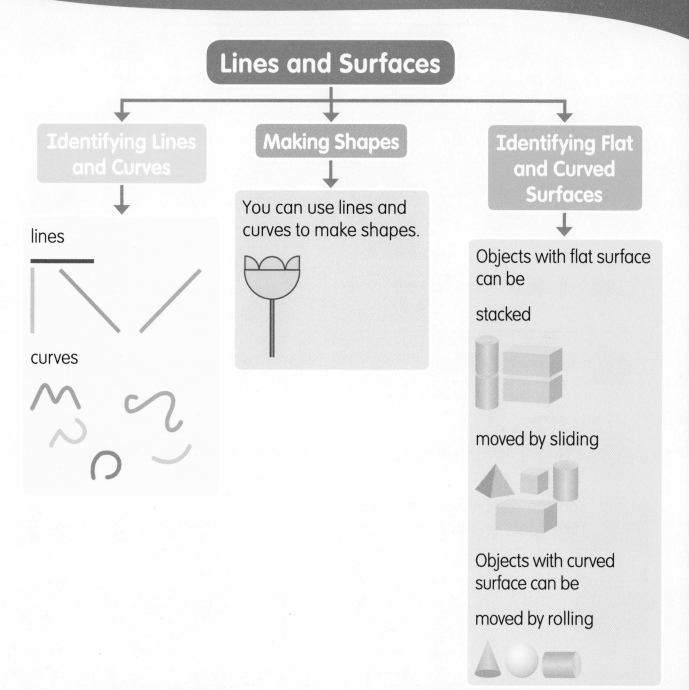

Shapes

Flat Shapes

a There are more flat shapes.

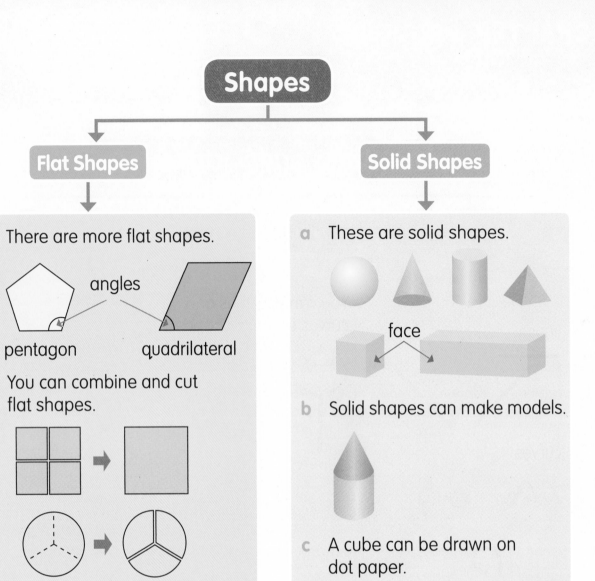

angles

pentagon   quadrilateral

b You can combine and cut flat shapes.

c You can combine shapes and take apart figures.

d Figures can be drawn on dot paper or square paper.

Solid Shapes

a These are solid shapes.

face

b Solid shapes can make models.

c A cube can be drawn on dot paper.

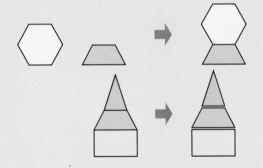
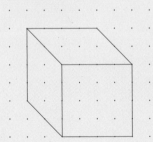
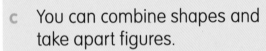

Name: _____ Date: _____

The picture is made up of lines and curves.
Answer each question.

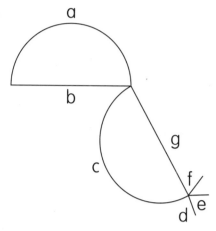

a   Which are lines? _____

b   Which are curves? _____

Draw the figure.

2   Draw a figure with 3 lines and 2 curves.

Look at the solid shapes.
Complete the table.
Then, answer each question.

cone   cylinder   sphere   cube

 a

Object	Number of Flat Surfaces	Number of Curved Surfaces
Cone		
Cylinder		
Sphere		
Cube		

b   Which solid shapes can stack?

_____

c   Which solid shapes can roll?

_____

d   Which solid shapes can slide?

_____

Count the flat shapes in the picture.
Complete the table.

4

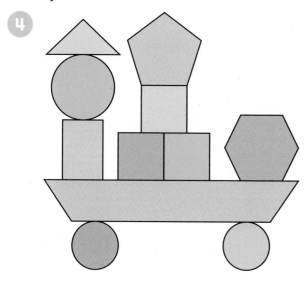

Flat Shape	Number of Flat Shapes
Rectangle	
Triangle	
Circle	
Square	
Trapezoid	
Hexagon	
Pentagon	

Draw lines to cut each shape into equal parts.
Then, color.

5 Show halves in two ways.
Then, color one half of the circle blue.

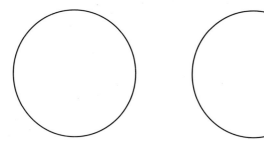

6 Show thirds in two ways.
Then, color one third of the rectangle red.

The figure is made up of three shapes.
Draw lines to show the shapes that make up the figure.
Then, name each shape.

7

_____

Draw a square.
Answer the question.

8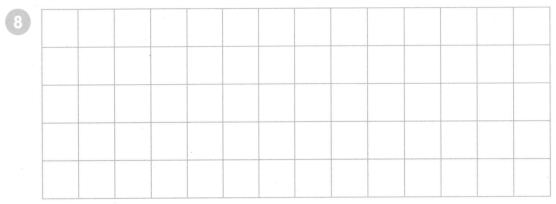

How many angles does it have? _____

Draw a shape with 1 less angle than a square.
Answer the question.

9

What shape is it? _____

Count the solid shapes in the model.
Then, complete the table.

10

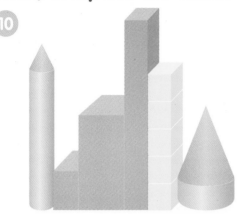

Solid Shape	Number of Solid Shapes
Cube	
Rectangular prism	
Cylinder	
Cone	

Answer each question.

11 Look at the solid shape.

a What is the solid shape? _____

b How many faces does the solid shape have? _____

c Which of the following shapes is a face of the solid shape?

_____

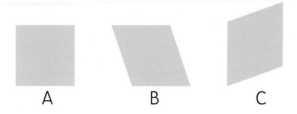

A   B   C

Assessment Prep

Answer each question.

12 Circle the solid shapes that make up the model.

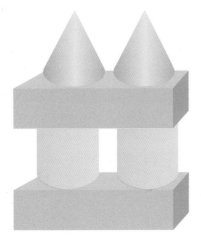

13 Draw a cube on the dot paper.

Name: _____ Date: _____

Playroom Fun

1 Naomi draws a picture of her toy teacup.
How many lines and curves does she use?

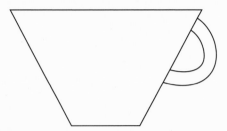

She uses _____ lines and _____ curves.

2 Naomi draws a square.
She cuts the square into 4 equal parts.
Then, she colors each part a different color.

a Use the square below to show what Naomi's square may look like.

b Circle the correct answer.
Each part is one third / fourth of the square.

3 Draw a figure with 4 lines and 2 curves.

4 Naomi has a solid shape.

a Count the number of flat surfaces and curved surfaces the block has.

The block has _____ flat surfaces and _____ curved surfaces.

b Which solid shapes have the same number of flat surfaces as the block?
Circle them.

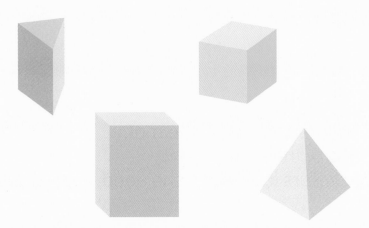

Will these solids roll? Why?

c   Draw a cube on the dot paper.

5 Naomi has a rectangular play mat.
She pastes some square stickers on the mat.
Each square sticker is of the same size.
How many square stickers in all does she need to cover the whole mat?

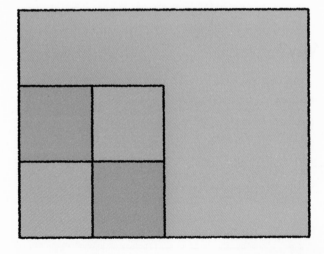

She needs _____ square stickers in all to cover the whole mat.

Rubric

Point(s)	Level	My Performance
7–8	4	• Most of my answers are correct. • I show all my work correctly. • I explain my thinking clearly and completely.
5–6.5	3	• Some of my answers are correct. • I show some of my work correctly. • I explain my thinking clearly.
3–4.5	2	• A few of my answers are correct. • I show little work correctly. • I explain some of my thinking clearly.
0–2.5	1	• A few of my answers are correct. • I show little or no work. • I do not explain my thinking clearly.

Teacher's Comments

Paul Klee

Paul Klee was an artist and a musician.
Colors were important in his work.
So were lines and geometric shapes.

Task

Self-Portrait

Work in pairs.

1. Use a colored paper to cut flat shapes with different lines, curves, and sides.

2. Use a marker to draw a self-portrait on a piece of art paper.

3. Put glue onto your self-portrait.

4. Cover your self-portrait with shapes.

5. Share your work.
Talk about the shapes you used.
Make a class art wall.

Glossary

A

- **after**

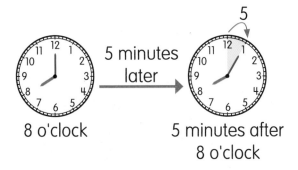

8 o'clock   5 minutes later →   5 minutes after 8 o'clock

- **A.M.**

  Use A.M. to talk about time just after midnight to just before noon.

  I get up each day at 7 A.M.

- **angle**

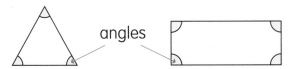

angles

A triangle has 3 angles.
A rectangle has 4 angles.

- **axis**

  An axis is a grid line that can be either vertical or horizontal.

  See **horizontal axis** and **vertical axis**.

B

- **bills**

C

- **clock face**

  This is a clock face.
  The short hand tells the hour.
  The long hand tells the minutes after the hour.

curve

Each of these drawings is a curve.

D

divide

Put into equal groups or share equally.

$6 \div 2 = 3$

Divide 6 toy cars into 3 equal groups of 2 toy cars.

division sentence

$15 \div 3 = 5$ is a division sentence.

dollar ($)

$20.00

dollar sign

decimal point

A decimal point separates the cents from the dollars.

$10.15

decimal point

dot paper

A dot paper shows a set of dots in equal rows and equal columns.

It shows 3 rows of 2.

E

equal groups

Having the same amount in each group.

© 2020 Marshall Cavendish Education Pte Ltd

equal parts

This rectangle is divided into three equal parts.
Each part is the same size.

even number

A number that divides exactly by 2.

F

face

Each flat surface of a solid is called a face.

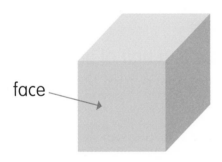

face

figure

You can make a figure by combining different plane shapes.

hexagon   trapezoid

H

horizontal bar graph

A horizontal bar graph is a chart with horizontal rectangular bars of lengths proportional to the values that they represent.

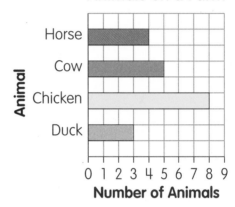

Animals on a Farm

horizontal axis

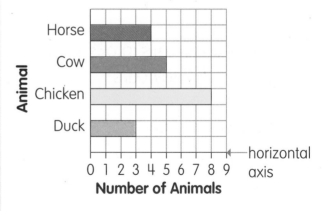

Animals on a Farm

horizontal axis

The value of the bars can be read from the horizontal axis, which is marked 0, 1, 2, 3, 4, 5, 6, 7, 8, and 9.

See **axis**.

hour

Hour is a unit of time equal to 60 minutes.

line plot

A line plot shows data on a number line.

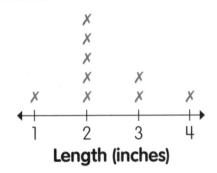

Length (inches)

Key: Each x stands for 1 leaf.

line

Each of these drawings is a line.

multiply

Put all the equal groups together.

There are 5 eggs in each group.
There are 2 groups.
$5 \times 2 = 10$
There are 10 eggs in all.

multiplication sentence

$3 \times 3 = 9$ is a multiplication sentence.

minute

Minute is a unit of time.
60 minutes equal to 1 hour.

odd number

A number that does not divide exactly by 2.

P

- **pentagon**

  A pentagon is a plane shape that has five sides.

- **P.M.**

  Use P.M. to talk about time just after noon to just before midnight.

  At 7:00 P.M. I watch my favorite T.V. show.

Q

- **quadrilateral**

  A quadrilateral is a plane shape that has four sides.

  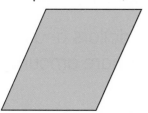

R

- **repeated addition**

  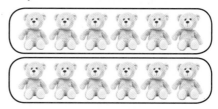

  You can use repeated addition to find the number of toy bears.

  $6 + 6 = 12$

  Groups of 6 are added 2 times.

  See **equal groups**.

- **repeated subtraction**

  You can use repeated subtraction to find the number of groups.

  $6 - 2 - 2 - 2 = 0$

  Groups of 2 are subtracted 3 times.

  See **equal groups**.

- **related multiplication facts**

  These are related multiplication facts.

  $3 \times 4 = 12$
  $4 \times 3 = 12$

- **related multiplication and division facts**

  These are related multiplication and division facts.

  $3 \times 2 = 6$ $6 \div 2 = 3$
  $2 \times 3 = 6$ $6 \div 3 = 2$

S

- **scale**

  A scale is the numbers that run along the vertical or horizontal axis of a graph.

  See **horizontal axis** and **vertical axis**.

- **survey**

  A survey is a method of collecting information or data.

- **share equally**

  Divide into equal groups.

- **skip count**

  Skip count by 2s:

  2   4   6   8   10

  Skip count by 5s:

  5   10   15   20   25

  Skip count by 10s:

  10   20   30   40   50

T

- **table**

  You can use a table to organize data in rows and columns.

  You can use dollars and cents tables to compare amounts of money.

	Dollars	Cents
Natalie	40	35
Emilia	40	80
Michael	44	55

$44.55 is the greatest amount.
$40.35 is the least amount.

Michael has the greatest amount of money.
Natalie has the least amount of money.

- **times**

  See **multiply**.

- **third of**

  Each part is one third of the circle.

- **thirds**

  3 thirds make a whole.

V ─────────────────

- **vertical bar graph**

  A vertical bar graph is a chart with vertical rectangular bars of lengths proportional to the values that they represent.

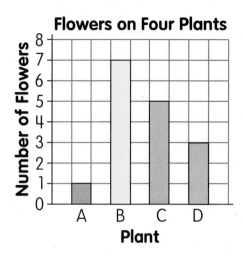

- **vertical axis**

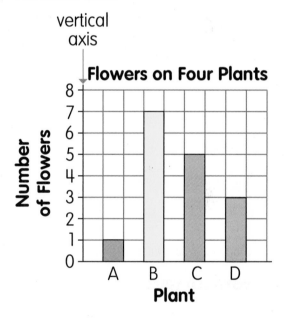

  The value of the bars can be read from the vertical axis, which is marked 0, 1, 2, 3, 4, 5, 6, 7, and 8.

  See **axis**.

Index

A

Addition
    equal groups, 52, 54, 57, 102–103, 106
    finding numbers in pattern by, 100, 108, 112, 198
    repeated, *see* Repeated addition

After, **205**–209, 211, 265–266

A.M., **214**–220, 263, 266, 275–277

Amounts of money
    comparing, 240–244, 264, 269, 272
    counting, 202, 227–228, 232, 264
    greatest, 239, 241–242, 244, 269, 272
    writing, 229–234, 236–238, 264

Angles, *throughout, see for example,* **312**, 315–316, 337, 342, 346

Attribute block tray
    Manipulatives, 299, 308

Axis, **17**

B

Bar graphs, *throughout, see for example,* 17–18, 20–24, 35, 40, 48
    making, 16, 19–21
        collecting data to, 19
    pictorial representations, *throughout, see for example,* 17–18, 21–24, 33, 40, 42–43
    reading, 16–18, 20

Bar models, *throughout, see for example,* 246–247, 251, 253, 260, 270
    pictorial representations, 246–253, 264

Bills, **222**–230, 235–237, 264, 267–268, 273–274
    recognizing and values, 222–223, 264

Blue counters,
    Manipulatives, 71, 156, 177

Blue cubes,
    Manipulatives, 65, 73, 115, 119

C

Cents, *throughout, see for example,* 200, 226, 229–234, 237–238, 264
    compare, 240–244, 264
    exchange for dollars, 231
    write amount as, 229–238

Circle, 280, 300, 305, 308

Clock, *throughout, see for example,* 203, 205, 219, 259, 272
    Manipulatives, 203, 206, 208

Clock face, **204**

Coins
    combining, 202
    exchanging, 201
    types, 200
    writing the value of, 200

Coin set, *throughout, see for example,* 221, 224, 229, 232, 239

Combine
    coins, 202
    and cut flat shapes, 303–304, 306, 342
    shapes and take apart figures, 308, 310, 342

Comparing
    amounts of money, 240–244, 264
        from least to greatest, 242, 269
        from greatest to least, 241, 244, 269, 272

Comparison models
    real-world problems, 250–251

Cone, 282, 294, 298, 323–325, 334

Connecting cubes,
    Manipulatives, 73, 115, 145

> Pages in **boldface** type show where a term is introduced.

© 2020 Marshall Cavendish Education Pte Ltd

Picture graphs, 2–3, 5–14, 16, 36–38, 40–41, 47
    making, 8–11
        collecting data to, 2, 10
    pictorial representations, *throughout, see for example*, 2–3, 5, 12–13, 36–38, 40–41
    reading, 8–11

P.M., **214**–215, 263

Pyramid, 282, 323–324

Quadrilaterals, **300**, 317, 322, 342

Real-world problems
    division, 85–86, 88, 90, 102
    money, 246–247, 250–251, 264
        and comparison models, 250–251
        and part-whole models, 246–247
    multiplication, 85–86, 88, 90, 102

Rectangles, *throughout, see for example*, 280, 300, 307–308, 312, 334

Rectangular prism, *throughout, see for example*, 282, 285, 323–325, 328–329, 334

Red counters,
    Manipulatives, 70–71, 115, 175

Red cubes,
    Manipulatives, 73, 94–95, 115

Related multiplication and division facts, **178**

Related multiplication facts, **169**, 170, 178

Repeated addition, **54**, 56, 107, 115, 127

Repeated subtraction, **71**–74, 108
    division, 71–75

Scale, **17**, 40

Shapes, 283, 299, 337–338, 342
    into equal parts, 305–306
    flat, *see* Flat shapes
    make figures using, 309–310

solid, *see* Solid shapes
    using lines and curves to make, 287–289

Sharing equally, **66**–67, 102

Skip counting, **116**
    by adding, *throughout, see for example*, 118, 128, 138, 147, 157
    by 2s, 116, 118, 124, 187
        dot paper, **117**
            pictorial representations, *throughout, see for example*, 117–121, 123, 125, 169, 187
    by 3s, 145–147, 152, 188
        dot paper
        pictorial representations, 146–151, 153, 170, 188
    by 4s, 157–159, 166, 188
        dot paper
        pictorial representations, *throughout, see for example*, 158–159, 161–163, 165–167, 171, 188
    by 5s, 127–128, 130, 134, 187, 198
        dot paper
            pictorial representations, *throughout, see for example*, 129, 131, 133–134, 169, 187
        to tell the time, 204–207, 263
        using hundreds chart, 127
    by 10s, 137–138, 140, 144, 187, 198
        dot paper
            pictorial representations, *throughout, see for example*, 139, 141, 143, 171, 187
        using hundreds chart, 137

Smaller than, 185

Solid shapes, *throughout, see for example*, 285, 290, 329, 334, 342
    counting, 328, 335, 347
    identifying, 282
    make models using, 323–327, 335, 342, 348

Sphere, 282, 323–324, 328, 334, 344

Square grid paper
    drawing figures, 312–315, 342

Squares, *throughout, see for example*, 280, 306–308, 315, 328–331, 338–339

Subtraction
    finding numbers in pattern by, 198
    repeated, *see* Repeated subtraction

Surfaces, 341
    curved, *see* Curved surfaces
    flat, *see* Flat surfaces

Survey, **8**, 10

Tables, *throughout, see for example,* **240**, 243, 297, 302, 310
    pictorial representations, *throughout, see for example,* 28, 156, 227, 311, 328

Tally chart, *throughout, see for example,* 3–11, 19–20, 28, 35, 42
    make picture graph, 6, 11
    pictorial representations, *throughout, see for example,* 3, 15–16, 26, 33, 42

Tangram, 339

10s
    skip counting by, 138, 140, 144, 187
        using hundreds chart, 137

Third of, **305**, 345, 349

Thirds, **305**, 307, 319, 340, 345

3s
    skip counting by, 145, 147, 152, 188

Times, **54**
    reading, 263
    showing, 206
    skip counting
        by 5s to tell the, 204, 206–207, 263
    telling, 199, 206
        in hours and minutes, 208, 210
    using A.M. and P.M., 214, 218, 263
    writing, 199, 263
        in hours and minutes, 208, 210

Transparent counters, Manipulatives, 53, 56, 66, 71, 85

Trapezoid, *throughout, see for example,* 280, 300, 304, 308–309, 317

Triangles, *throughout, see for example,* 280, 308, 312, 317, 345

2-digit number, 185

2s
    skip counting by, 116, 118, 124, 187

Vertical bar graph, **17**, 40

Writing
    amount
        in cents, 232, 234, 238, 269
        in dollars, 232, 234, 238, 269
        of money, 229–230, 232–233, 264
    time, 199, 219, 265
        in hours and minutes, 208–210
    value of coins, 200
    value of bills, 223, 235, 267

Yellow counters, Manipulatives, 71, 175

Yellow cubes, Manipulatives, 73

Photo Credits

xiib: © MCE. Objects sponsored by Noble International Pte Ltd., xiib: © MCE, 1tl: © RiverNorthPhotography/iStock, 1tl: © Ron Zmiri/Shutter Stock, 1tm: © merkur/Shutter Stock, 1tm: © Antoninapotapenko/iStock, 1tr: © YinYang/iStock, 1b: © rvimages/iStock, 35: Created by Fwstudio - Freepik.com, 51t: © onurdongel/iStock, 51tm: © BALDARI/iStock, 51tm: © Es sarawuth/Shutter Stock, 51tr: © August_0802/Shutter Stock, 51ml: © maytih/iStock, 51b: © All For You/Shutter Stock, 53b: © MCE, 54: © rotsukhon lam/Shutter Stock, 55t: © rotsukhon lam/Shutter Stock, 56m: © MCE, 60: © piotr_pabijan/Shutter Stock, 65b: © MCE. Objects sponsored by Noble International Pte Ltd., 66: © MCE, 69b: © Igor Kovalchuk/123rf.com, 70t: © MCE, 70m: © Niklef3/Dreamstime.com, 70b: © Chinnasorn Pangcharoen/Dreamstime.com, 71t: © MCE, 71b: © Elphotographo/Dreamstime.com, 72t: © Elphotographo/Dreamstime.com, 73t: © Photozek07/Think Stock/iStock, 73b: © MCE. Objects sponsored by Noble International Pte Ltd., 74b: © Brian Jackson/123rf.com, 75b: © voyata/123rf.com, 76t: © andreahast/123rf.com, 76m: © belchonock/123rf.com, 76b: © Julián Rovagnati/Dreamstime.com, 78t: © Tanapon Samphao/Dreamstime.com, 78b: © Wachira sonwongsa/123rf.com, 80t: © Phive2015/Dreamstime.com, 80b: © Nikolai Sorokin/Dreamstime.com, 83m: © Brian Jackson/123rf.com, 84t: © Aliaksei Smalenski/Dreamstime.com, 84m: © Vladimir Nenov/123rf.com, 84b: © Benjamin Roesngsamran/123rf.com, 85m: © MCE, 86b: © Photozek07/Think Stock/iStock, 89: © Vadim Petrov/Dreamstime.com, 90: © piotr_pabijan/Shutter Stock, 92: © Tinarayna/Dreamstime.com, 93m: © MCE. Objects sponsored by Noble International Pte Ltd., 93m: © Chinnasorn Pangcharoen/Dreamstime.com, 93b: © bergamont/Shutter Stock, 94b: © MCE. Objects sponsored by Noble International Pte Ltd., 95t: © MCE. Objects sponsored by Noble International Pte Ltd., 96b: © MCE, 97t: © Riccardo Adelini/Dreamstime.com, 97b: © Yvdavyd/Dreamstime.com, 99: Created by Fwstudio - Freepik.com, 102ml: © rotsukhon lam/Shutter Stock, 102mr: © Chinnasorn Pangcharoen/Dreamstime.com, 102mr: © bergamont/Shutter Stock, 102bm: © Igor Kovalchuk/123rf.com, 104t: © Petr Malyshev/Dreamstime.com, 104t: © MCE, 108m: © Edgaras Kurauskas/Dreamstime.com, 110tr: © Eric Isselee/123rf.com, 110mr: © Artsiom Petrushenka/123rf.com, 111: © Katarzyna Białasiewicz/123rf.com, 111bl: © Panithan Fakseemuang/123rf.com, 111bm: © Panithan Fakseemuang/123rf.com, 111br: © Panithan Fakseemuang/123rf.com, 113t: © kitzcorner/Shutter Stock, 113b: © Richard Peterson/Shutter Stock, 114t: © Danny Kosmayer/123rf.com, 114b: © Stacy Barnett/123rf.com, 115m: © MCE, 115b: © MCE. Objects sponsored by Noble International Pte Ltd., 117t: © sashkin7/123rf.com, 117t: © Markus Mainka/123rf.com, 118t: © Popa Ion Adrian/123rf.com, 118m: © utima/123rf.com, 118b: © Maxim Loskutnikov/123rf.com, 119t: © MCE. Objects sponsored by Noble International Pte Ltd., 120b: © robbiverte/Think Stock/iStock , 120b: © Paperkites/Think Stock/iStock, 122: © piotr_pabijan/Shutter Stock, 123t: © basketman23/123rf.com, 123m: © Mariusz Blach/123rf.com, 123b: © Yalçın Sonat/123rf.com, 129t: © ksushsh/123rf.com, 129m: © belchonock/123rf.com, 130t: © robbiverte/Think Stock/iStock , 130t: © Paperkites/Think Stock/iStock, 132: © piotr_pabijan/Shutter Stock, 134t: © Bartas Miklasevicius/123rf.com, 139t: © kritchanut/123rf.com, 139t: © serezniy/123rf.com, 139m: © Nisakorn Neera/123rf.com, 140t: © robbiverte/Think Stock/iStock, 140t: © Paperkites/Think Stock/iStock, 140b: © Anuwat Susomwong/123rf.com, 142: © piotr_pabijan/Shutter Stock, 145t: © MCE. Objects sponsored by Noble International Pte Ltd., 146t: © Pisut Chuanyoo/123rf.com, 146m: © Phanuwat Nandee/123rf.com, 147t: © Vladimir Nenov/123rf.com, 149b: © robbiverte/Think Stock/iStock, 149b: © Paperkites/Think Stock/iStock, 156: © MCE, 158t: © Brian Jackson/123rf.com, 158m: © madllen/123rf.com, 159b: © Fernando Gregory Milan/123rf.com, 162b: © robbiverte/Think Stock/iStock, 162b: © Paperkites/Think Stock/iStock, 164: © piotr_pabijan/Shutter Stock, 165t: © bsauter/123rf.com, 165m: © Igor Stramyk/123rf.com, 170: © olegdudko/123rf.com, 171b: © Timmary/123rf.com, 172t: © Marcin Twardosz/123rf.com, 172b: © Viktar Malyshchyts/123rf.com, 173b: © Phanuwat Nandee/123rf.com, 174t: © Gergana Valkova/123rf.com, 175m: © MCE, 176m: © Monica-photo/Think Stock/iStock, 176b: © sashkin7/123rf.com, 176b: © Markus Mainka/123rf.com, 177b: © MCE, 178t: © rotsukhon lam/Shutter Stock, 178t: kritchanut/123rf.com, 181m: © Markus Mainka/123rf.com, 183: Created by Fwstudio - Freepik.com, 183t: © Phanuwat Nandee/123rf.com, 189m: © voyata/123rf.com, 192t: © Wanich Sirilon/123rf.com, 193t: ©

© 2020 Marshall Cavendish Education Pte Ltd

Published by Marshall Cavendish Education
Times Centre, 1 New Industrial Road, Singapore 536196
Customer Service Hotline: (65) 6213 9688
US Office Tel: (1-914) 332 8888 | Fax: (1-914) 332 8882
E-mail: cs@mceducation.com
Website: www.mceducation.com

Distributed by
Houghton Mifflin Harcourt
125 High Street
Boston, MA 02110
Tel: 617-351-5000
Website: www.hmhco.com/programs/math-in-focus

First published 2020

ISBN 978-0-358-10180-2

Printed in Singapore

2 3 4 5 6 7 8   1401   25 24 23 22 21 20
4500799763   B C D E F

The cover image shows a Pygmy slow loris.
These animals can be found in Southeast Asia.
They live in forests and feed on insects, tree parts, and fruit.
A Pygmy slow loris has a round head, narrowed nose and big forward-facing eyes.
It only comes out at night.
Its big eyes help it to find food in the dark.